THE MARR STORY

The History of a Fishing Family

Compiled by

Michael Thompson

J. MARR LTD.
1995

Published by
J. Marr Ltd.,
St. Andrew's Dock,
Hull HU3 4PN

Distributed by
The Hutton Press,
130 Canada Drive, Cherry Burton,
Beverley HU17 7SB

Printed and bound by
Clifford Ward & Co. (Bridlington) Ltd.,
55 West Street, Bridlington,
East Yorkshire YO15 3DZ

ISBN   1 872167 69 1

CONTENTS

FOREWORD

I have greatly enjoyed assisting Michael Thompson to put together this record of our family's involvement with the deep water fishing industry both nationally and inter-nationally.

The account spans the rise and decline of the once great Distant Water fishing industries in the U.K.

My sons and I felt that the record should be set down before memories faded.

I would like to thank all those who have assisted with the records of both the family and the Company. In particular Harold Davison, John Panton, Howard Baker of Write Angles, James Hind, Tony Lofthouse, Arthur Credland of the Kingston upon Hull Town Docks Museum, also the staff of the Kingston upon Hull Records Office and the staff of the Hull Central Library, Hull City Libraries.

I hope you enjoy browsing through this document as much as we have enjoyed putting it together.

G. Alan Marr, C.B.E.
March 1995

ACKNOWLEDGEMENTS

J. Marr Ltd. would like to thank the following concerns for their kind permission to use their copyright photographs in this book:-

Fotoflite, Littlestone Road, New Romney, Kent.
The Town Docks Museum, Hull City Council.
Innes Studios, The Square, Hessle.
Peter Horsley, Lord Street, Fleetwood.
David Buckley, Fleetwood.
Malcolm Fussey, Hull.
Brian Milns, Hull.
Colin Nicoll, Hull.

Joseph Marr 1835-1900
Fish merchant, snack owner, steam trawler owner.

Chapter 1:
ORIGINS AND EARLY YEARS

William Marr was born in Dundee in 1808. As a young man he settled in Hull having found employment in the port's whaling trade as a harpooner, work which suited his stature, William being 6′3″ tall in his stocking feet. Whilst in Hull he met Rachel Wood whose parents Oswald and Charlotte Wood owned the Masons Arms public house at 22 Chapel Lane, off Lowgate. William and Rachel were married in the Parish of Drypool in 1833, the couple lived at the Masons Arms with Rachel's parents.

Hunting whales was difficult and dangerous work, often undertaken in harsh weather conditions and a high cost was paid in the loss of ships and men. The whaling seasons of 1835-1836 were particularly disastrous, due to a scarcity of whales and the presence of massive fields of thick ice. Several vessels were trapped and crushed. The crews endured great hardship in the cruel climate, many dying of scurvy and frostbite. William Marr was one such victim; while sailing in the 1835 expedition he fell ill and died and was buried at Greenland, never knowing that his wife had given birth to a son on 16th October 1835. Rachel was just 21 years old when she was widowed, and the son that William would never see was christened Joseph.

Subsequently Rachel remarried in 1841, to a fish merchant named William Elder, and the family set up home at No. 6 Alfred Street, in Hull. Despite this element of security Joseph's early years must have been difficult, for this was the period that would become infamous as "The Hungry Forties". At the age of 18 he set out to make his fortune travelling to Australia where he spent several years searching for gold at the Ballerat gold fields. Eventually Joseph returned home to Hull, where he met and fell in love with Ann Stephenson. His hope was that Ann would return with him to Australia but she did not favour the idea, and ultimately he decided to settle in Hull.

Joseph married Ann in 1862, when he was 27 and she was just 19. In 1860 Joseph rented two smoking kilns in the Dairycoates district of Hull and commenced business as a fish curer; a trade he

*The Hull whaler **Diana** at Greenland. From a painting by J. Wheldon.*

had learned from his step-father. The venture proved successful and soon Joseph purchased his own curing houses. He also now acquired the first family home, at No. 21 St. Mark's Square, off St. James Street. Later however, he transferred the family to No. 4 Vauxhall Grove, Hessle Road, a location closer to their fish curing premises.

Subsequently Joseph extended his operations, and in 1870 became the owner of a newly-built fishing smack which he named *Adelaide* — a reflection of his continuing love for Australia. During the fifteen years that followed he purchased a further six vessels: the *Earl of Mar* in 1873, *Rachel Anne* in 1875, *Edith Louise* in 1880, *Emily Florence* in 1881, *Amy Isobel* in 1883 and *Lillian Maude* in 1885. All were newly built vessels, the last five being named after Joseph and Ann's daughters. Later Joseph acquired two second-hand smacks: the *Mascotte* in 1886 and the *Argument* in 1889. The fleet represented a substantial investment at that time; in the 1870's fishing smacks cost between £700 and £800 to build and fit-out ready for sea, and this had increased to £1900 by the 1890's.

In all Joseph and Ann had eleven children: five girls and six boys. William was born in 1864, Rachel Anne in 1865, Joseph Arthur in 1867, James Herbert in 1869, David in 1872, Frederick Robert in 1874, Edith Louise in 1875, Walter Henry in 1878, Emily Florence in 1880, Amy Isobel in 1882 and Lillian Maude in 1884. Sadly Frederick died in infancy, and further tragedy would befall the family in September 1885 when both David and Walter died from typhoid fever.

By the 1870's Joseph had moved his family to No. 35 Nile Street, a select area close to the docks. It was from here that the business was run, with the dining room serving also as an office. The family became accustomed to clearing the table when it was needed for business purposes, which was a regular occurrence; the crews from the smacks received their settlements about every nine or ten weeks and would visit the Nile Street house to receive payment.

The fishing season was divided into two parts, the summer and the winter. The summer season was generally of three months duration and during this period the smacks fished in fleets, their catches being taken to the various markets by fast sailing smacks known as cutters. In the winter the smacks fished singly, with trips averaging 14 to 21 days.

On their return to port for stores the smacks would land fish at the Hull market. This was sold by auction under the supervision of the smack owner, or a salesman appointed by him. This trend continues to the present day.

The 1870's were times of expansion for the Hull fishing trade.

By 1878 nearly 400 smacks were fishing from the port, and this would rise to a peak of 448 in 1887. Some of the smack owners were local men like Joseph Marr but many others had settled from other ports, particularly Brixham. Inevitably there was a certain amount of friction between the 'natives' and the 'foreigners'.

By the early 1890's Joseph Marr was feeling the effects of a strenuous life. He had provided his son Joseph Arthur with fish curing premises and a house of his own in Vauxhall Grove in which to reside with his wife Annie Witty, whom he had married in 1889. The eldest son, William, had been badly injured in an accident as a child. Thus only James Herbert was left to enter the business, and he was studying dentistry. However, as his father's health deteriorated James abandoned dentistry and entered the business full-time, and soon the main responsibility for running the company rested with him and his mother Ann.

Around this time the new steam-powered trawlers began to enter service, their arrival provoking conflicting responses. Some of the fishing smack owners felt that the new vessels were of no use to the fishing industry and could never replace the fishing smacks. At that time there was not a vast difference in construction costs between the sailing smacks and the steam trawlers, but the operating costs of the latter were higher; they required larger crews, needed coal for fuel and were more expensive to maintain and repair. Such drawbacks were, however, balanced by a major advantage; steam trawlers could fish when there was little or no wind, unlike the sailing smacks which needed a half-gale to operate efficiently.

Ignoring the sceptics Joseph and James chose to invest in the new technology, and in 1891 they built their first steam trawler, proudly naming it *Marrs*. Gradually the Marr smacks were sold or scrapped and replaced by steam trawlers, with the last two smacks being sold in 1902. The wisdom of the Marr family's decision to adopt steam soon became apparent; many of the owners who had clung tenaciously to sail went bankrupt and vanished, and by 1903 all the Hull smack fleet was gone.

In 1895 James Herbert Marr married Mary Ann Edwards, and subsequently became the father of three sons — Alan and twins Leslie and Geoffrey — and one daughter, Evelyn Mary. In this mid-1890's period, too, James appears to have become restless. He was not on the best of terms with some of the other Hull trawler owners, and was attracted to the developing fishing port of Fleetwood, on the Lancashire coast. Accordingly, in 1898, he moved to Fleetwood with a fleet of three steam trawlers; *Marrs* and *Rattler*, both built in 1891, and *Lucerne* built in 1896. By 1900 this fleet had been reinforced by the *Annie*, built in 1898, and the

An artist's impression of St. Andrew's Dock circa 1895.

Akranes, built in 1899. Several key members of the shore and seagoing staff accompanied James to Fleetwood, no doubt attracted both by the challenge of establishing the company in a new location and the opportunity of moving their families to a new town cleaner than the large industrial city of Hull.

The arrival of the small fleet in 1898 was welcomed in Fleetwood, for the previous year the port had lost the business of the 32-strong Kelsall & Beeching fleet when the company returned to Hull. In the years that followed the J. Marr fleet was to expand and play a major role in Fleetwood's development as a fishing port.

James established an office for the company — now known as J. Marr & Son — in the Old Custom House Building in Dock Street, Fleetwood, and took residence with his family at No. 143 Promenade Road, Fleetwood. Soon afterwards he developed a friendship with James Alexander Robertson, one of the sons of James Robertson who owned a flourishing engineering business in Fleetwood. James found the engineering knowledge of his new friend invaluable, and subsequently James Alexander Robertson joined the business, eventually becoming a shareholder and director.

In the 1890's, with the family business in competent hands, Joseph Marr retired to Bridlington to enjoy the fashionable Victorian practice of 'taking the sea air'. The family moved to 'Oakleigh', No. 2 Bessingby Road, Bridlington, and at the same time acquired No. 423 Beverley Road, Hull, which was to prove a useful business and social residence.

Joseph Marr died on 28th June 1900. Following his death the enterprise he had created continued as a partnership between James and his mother until 29th May 1902 when it was transformed into a limited company under the title 'J. Marr & Son Limited'. The 'J' referred to Joseph Marr, the 'son' being Joseph Arthur. James and his mother chose to retain that same name for the company as a respect for its late founder.

The inaugural meeting of the Company was held on 16th June 1902. At this meeting James Herbert Marr was appointed chairman, James Alexander Robertson was appointed as a director and Peter Johnson was appointed secretary. A year later, on 6th June 1903, Peter Johnson resigned as secretary and Edward Towne was appointed in his place.

In that year of 1903, too, the family suffered the loss of their eldest daughter, Rachel Anne, who died at the age of 38. A successful businesswoman, Rachel Anne Boheme owned two ladies fashion shops on Beverley Road. As a result of this untimely death Rachel's daughter, Annie Teresa — known as 'Cusan' —was brought up by her aunts.

THE ORIGINAL SHAREHOLDERS OF J. MARR & SON LTD.

Names, Addresses, and Descriptions of Subscribers	Number of Shares taken by each Subscriber
JAMES HERBERT MARR, Custom House, Fleetwood, Fish Merchant.	One
ANN MARR, 423 Beverley Road, Hull, Widow.	One
JOSEPH ARTHUR MARR, 58 Eastbourne Street, Hull, Fish Merchant.	One
MARY ANN MARR, 143 Promenade Road, Fleetwood, Married Woman.	One
JAMES ALEXANDER ROBERTSON, Dock Street, Fleetwood, Engineer.	One
JOHN THOMAS HILL, Quay Road, Bridlington, Dentist.	One
PETER JOHNSON, 58 North Church Street, Fleetwood, Secretary.	One

Dated the 27th day of May, 1902.

WITNESS to the signatures of James Herbert Marr, Mary Ann Marr, James Alexander Robertson and Peter Johnson.

WILLIAM SWARBRICK,
Assist. Railway Supt.,
36 Kingston Terrace,
Fleetwood.

WITNESS to the signatures of Ann Marr, Joseph Arthur Marr, and John Thomas Hill.

HERBERT WOODHOUSE,
Solicitor,
8 Parliament Street,
Hull.

James Herbert Marr.
Chairman of J. Marr & Son Ltd.
1902 – 1916.

James Alexander Robertson.
A brilliant marine engineer, he was one of the founder members of
J. Marr & Son Ltd.

Chapter 2:
FLEETWOOD AND THE FIRST WORLD WAR

In the early days of Fleetwood traditional fish such as cod and haddock were considered to be the significant catches. Hake also found its way into the nets but it was largely regarded as not worth bringing to port, and so usually thrown overboard. James Marr was one of the few who realised the possibilities of the hake fishery and he worked hard to develop hake marketing in the Lancashire industrial towns. As a result hake came to be much appreciated by fish and chip shops as a good, cheap, solid fish, and gradually the hake fishery became a major element in the prosperity of Fleetwood. The majority of hake were to be found off the north-west coast of Scotland and the west coast of Ireland, and the catches were supplemented by the more traditional cod and haddock netted around Rockall and Faroe.

The early years of any company are seldom easy, and J. Marr & Son Limited was no exception in this respect; the accounts of those times show little in the way of surplus money. By 1906, however, the fleet had increased to seven trawlers, with the purchase of the *Nile* FD11 in 1902, and the *Amy* FD39 and the *Maude* FD40, both built in 1905. The *Annie* was sold out of the fleet in 1905. In 1906 James Robertson and James Marr formed the Lancashire Steam Fishing Co. Ltd., and diversified into allied activities such as curing, salting and fish merchanting.

During this period the scale of commercial shipping operations through Fleetwood declined to such an extent that fishing vessels began landing their catches at the port's Wyre Dock. J. Marr and Son transferred to new purpose-built premises at No. 228 Dock Street, Fleetwood, and in 1908 James Herbert Marr was instrumental in the founding of the Fylde Ice Company, which produced supplies of crushed ice for preserving fish in the holds of trawlers and in the local fish market.

By now the cost of building trawlers had escalated significantly, as the insured value of the Marr fleet in 1908 indicates:

Arkanes	FD33	built 1899	184 tons — £3,400
Diana	FD135	built 1899	172 tons — £2,850
Evelyn	FD59	built 1906	235 tons — £5,700
Lucerne	FD34	built 1896	154 tons — £2,400
Mary	FD84	built 1906	256 tons — £6,450
Nile	FD11	built 1896	196 tons — £2,650
Rattler	FD199	built 1891	149 tons — £1,700

Despite such costs 61 steam trawlers were registered at Fleetwood in that year, and within twelve months those owned by the Tettenhall Steam Fishing Company and Norbreck Steam Fishing Company had passed into the control of James Marr.

These two companies had been formed in 1905 by individuals from outside the industry who had surplus capital to invest in eight new trawlers. By 1909 both companies were struggling, and James Marr was invited to take over their complete management. This arrangement continued until the First World War, when all eight trawlers were chartered by the Government. At the end of hostilities the two companies went into voluntary liquidation, with no loss of capital.

At the eighth annual general meeting of J. Marr & Son Ltd., on 22nd April 1910, Joseph Arthur Marr was appointed director of the company, and moved from Hull to Fleetwood to join his brother. By now he was the father of seven children; Joseph Arthur, David, James, Harry, Frank, Lilly and Dolly. His fish curing business at 21 Witty Street, Hull, was retained until 1926, as was his property in Vauxhall Grove. According to legend Joseph Arthur was responsible for introducing a certain exotic element into the company's operations. It is said that while holidaying in the Mediterranean he found the christian names of the local ladies appealing, and adopted several of these as the 'name theme' for the company's trawlers.

In 1912 an associate company, The Active Fishing Company, was formed — essentially as a concern for the 'boys' of the Marr family. Senior staff of J. Marr & Son Ltd. were offered share participation in the new company and most took advantage of this. Five former Hull trawlers were purchased for the company, which took its name from one of these vessels.

By December 1913 the Company's fleet consisted of 32 trawlers, deployed as follows: J. Marr & Son, 12 vessels; Norbreck, 3 vessels; Tettenhall, 5 vessels; Lancashire, 5 vessels; Active, 7 vessels. In the Lloyds Register of Shipping for that year the Norbreck Steam Fishing Company and the Tettenhall Steam Fishing Company Ltd. appeared under the name of James Herbert Marr. The Lancashire Steam Fishing Company Ltd. and the Active Fishing Company Ltd. appeared under the name of James Alexander Robertson.

By 1914 the number of trawlers registered at Fleetwood exceeded 120, but this fleet was rapidly depleted following the outbreak of the First World War. The majority of these vessels were requisitioned by the Government for minesweeping and armed escort duties with the Royal Navy, and most of the crews went into naval service with their trawlers. During the course of the war 34 Fleetwood trawlers were lost, either on active service or while fishing.

Wyre Dock, Fleetwood, with commercial shipping around the turn of the century.

*Wyre Dock, Fleetwood circa 1908. The Marr trawler **Akranes** is receiving a supply of crushed ice from the Fylde Ice Company's premises on the dockside.*

The J. Marr & Son Ltd. fish landing staff.
It was the trawler owner's responsibility to land and sell his trawler's catch at the local fish market.
To this end a reliable team of workers was established to handle this work.

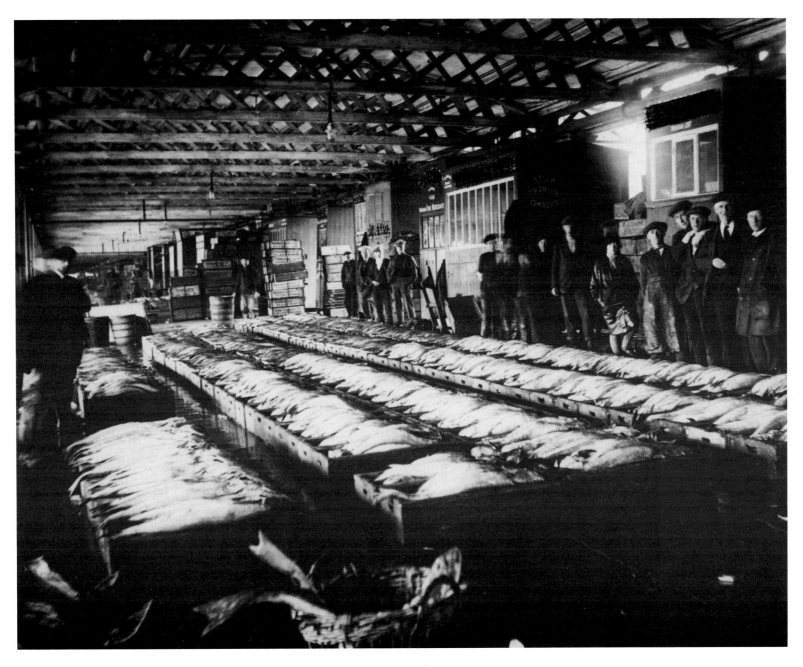

Fish laid out for auction on Fleetwood fish market.

*The **Velia** one of the eleven new trawlers ordered for the Company just prior to the 1914-1918 War.*

Wyre Dock Fleetwood 1915. Commercial shipping has once again returned to the port during the 1914-1918 War.

Prior to the outbreak of the War the Company had launched into an ambitious shipbuilding programme, placing orders for eleven new trawlers at prices ranging from £7,650 to £9,000. By the time hostilities commenced the *Imelda* FD13 (1914) had been commissioned and the *Lucida* FD20 (1914) had been delivered, but on completion the remaining nine vessels went straight from the builder's hands into war service. Of these, the *Idena* FD288 was sunk in 1918. As well as providing the Royal Navy with ships and crews the Company made considerable financial contributions to Britain's war effort through the purchase of Victory Bonds, Victory War Loans and similar Government instruments.

Only the Company's two older vessels, the *Rattler* FD199 and the *Fly* FD166, were retained as fishing units, and both continued to fish throughout the War. During the years of the conflict, however, the Company developed a considerable foreign agency with Icelandic trawler owners who landed their catches at Fleetwood. In addition it managed a considerable cargo trade between Fleetwood and Iceland, importing salt fish and fish products and exporting coal, salt and large quantities of general cargo. During this wartime period Fleetwood resumed its role as a commercial shipping port, with sailing ships and cargo steamers working general cargo at Wyre Dock. After the War the fishing industry would once again become the port's main source of work, and for many years it would rank as Britain's third largest fishing port.

On 4th November 1916 the Company suffered a great blow with the death of James Herbert Marr at the age of 47. He had fallen ill early in that year and had been admitted to a nursing home, where he was attended by his wife, mother and sisters. Before the end he wrote to Edward Towne requesting that he look after his boys, and Edward dutifully complied.

At that time James Herbert's son, Alan Marr, was overseas in the Forces, serving in one of the Fleetwood 'Pals' battalions. Accordingly James Herbert's widow, Mary Ann Marr, was appointed to the board, with Joseph Arthur Marr and James Alexander Robertson being appointed joint managing directors — the latter taking responsibility for the running of the company. Alan survived the War to return to civilian life, and in February 1919 he replaced his mother on the board as a director.

Upon the cessation of hostilities, in November 1918, the Government began to release vessels from charter and return them to their owners. Returning them to service was no simple matter, however, for in most cases several months of reconditioning was required before fishing operations could be resumed. The last Marr trawler to be released was the *Collena*

FD115 and it was not until the summer of 1920 that this vessel was able to steam forth and take up the task that had been so brutally interrupted by the coming of War.

Alan Marr, circa 1911.

Chapter 3:
THE DIFFICULT 'TWENTIES

The arrival of peace ushered in a boom period in Lancashire. Cotton millionaires were made overnight, and some pumped their surplus funds into the Fleetwood fishing industry. New companies mushroomed in this prosperous climate but few survived the reversal of fortune which followed. During the War years the Government had built large numbers of minesweeper trawlers, which had now become surplus. These were offered for sale at prices between £8,000 and £9,250, and were eagerly acquired by trawler owners keen to rebuild their fleets. Unfortunately the arrival of these vessels flooded the market, causing the British fishing fleet to become too large. This in turn precipitated a dramatic slump, making the 1920's a difficult period for the industry.

In 1924 Joseph Arthur Marr purchased four former Hull trawlers at a bargain price. Transferring them to Fleetwood he formed the Dinas Steam Trawler Company, operating this separately from J. Marr & Son with the assistance of his sons David and Joseph Arthur Jnr.

The Marr Company was passing through this difficult economic climate when it was struck by a number of personal setbacks, the first being the sudden death on 12th October 1924 of James Alexander Robertson. This event was doubly unfortunate as Alan Marr, who was appointed chairman on 16th October, was now seriously ill, and Leslie and Geoffrey Marr had only just entered the business. Accordingly Edward Towne, who had been secretary almost since the incorporation of the company, was appointed director.

The loss of James Alexander Robertson was a grievous blow to the Company. A member of one of Fleetwood's most prominent families, and a highly respected member of the local fishing community, he served effectively as chairman of the Fleetwood Fishing Vessel Owners Association and had been awarded the O.B.E. He had been responsible for the running of J. Marr & Son since the death of James Herbert Marr in 1916, and his contribution to the Company over the span of 23 years is inestimable.

On 30th May 1925 Leslie James Marr and his brother Geoffrey Edwards Marr were elected as directors. Then on 1st December 1925, Alan Marr died after a long and painful illness, at the age of 29. A week later Joseph Arthur Marr was appointed chairman; the management of the company now devolved largely on Edward Towne and Leslie and Geoffrey Marr.

The death of Alan Marr caused deep sadness throughout the local fishing community for he had often sailed on the Company's trawlers and was well-liked and respected by both seagoing and shore staff. During the First World War he had served with distinction as a despatch rider with the Royal Engineers, holding the rank of corporal and gaining the Distinguished Conduct Medal. It may possibly be that the harsh conditions he endured during that period were responsible for the subsequent illness which robbed him of his life at such an early age.

An earlier loss to the Company had been the senior director Mrs. Ann Marr, who had died in 1922. Despite this, a female influence on the company's operations was not lacking during this decade. It continued to be provided by Joseph Marr's daughters — Mrs. Edith Louise Shaw, Mrs. Emily Florence Swales, Mrs. Amy Isobel Panton and Mrs. Lillian Maude Hogarth — all of whom were active at shareholders' meetings and gave great support to the company's affairs.

As the 1920's progressed many trawler owners began to reorganise their fleets, replacing their older trawlers with new, larger vessels. Such was the depressed state of the second-hand market that many good vessels were available at reasonable prices, and the Company took the opportunity to acquire several of these, including the *Pelican* FD150 for £5,500, *Sir Mark Sykes* FD410 for £8,500, and the *Hiddenite* FD180 and *Avanturine* FD181 for £5,750 each.

One unique aspect of Marr's operations was the Company's maintenance of its own ships' stores, which obviated the need to rely upon ships' chandlers. For many years the store manager was Percy Edwards, a brother of Mary Ann Edwards. A butcher by trade, Percy was always on the look-out for a bargain and was an enthusiastic advocate of bulk buying. His enthusiasm for both forms of economy led to some disquiet when on one occasion he was offered pork at a low price. True to his beliefs he obtained a large quantity of the meat — and proceeded to supply it to the Company's trawlers in such relentless abundance that the skippers eventually threatened to change their religion in a bid to secure a more balanced diet!

In addition to its trawler fleet the Company had built up a substantial fish curing business at the salt fish farm at Copse Road. However, this enterprise began to decline during the 1920's, and had almost disappeared by the late 1930's.

The first cold storage accommodation was provided in 1927 by the Fylde Ice and Cold Storage Company, and was used largely for preserving kippers. Further accommodation was added in 1934, and to this day J. Marr Ltd. remain major shareholders in this concern.

On 1st April 1929 Joseph Arthur Marr retired from the board at the age of 62. He moved into offices purchased for the Dinas Company and devoted his time to running his own trawler and fish curing company. His position as chairman was taken by Geoffrey Edwards Marr, who was at that time only 25 years old, and Henry Atkinson was appointed secretary.

Fleetwood Dock in the 1930's.
*Berthed under the coal gantries is the Company's trawler **Teroma** FD17.*
*The **Teroma** was part of the Marr fleet between 1929-1953.*
During the 1939-45 War she served as a minesweeper with the Royal Navy, the role the vessel had originally been built for in 1918.

Chapter 4:
RETURNING TO HULL, AND TO WAR

The 1920's had been a difficult period for the fishing industry and a testing time for J. Marr & Son. The decade that followed was to prove equally challenging, and the Company was fortunate to have at its helm two young men as determined and energetic as Geoffrey and Leslie Marr.

Away from business Geoffrey was a keen yachtsman and also an enthusiastic golfer, and this latter interest led him to meet his future bride, Norah Smith. Norah's father owned the local pub at Knott End, where Geoffrey would occasionally play a round of golf. In 1930 Geoffrey and Norah were married, and subsequently had three children: Geoffrey Alan, Josephine and Susan.

Leslie Marr had rather the opposite experience, for in his case it was the courtship which prompted the pastime in which he was to excel. The young lady in question, Miss Stella Cooper, lived in Bournemouth, and as the courtship progressed during the late 1920's the inconvenience posed by the distance became increasingly apparent. Leslie resolved the problem, by purchasing an aeroplane, taking flying lessons and gaining his pilot's licence. He thereupon pursued the courtship by flying regularly from Squire's Gate, Blackpool, to the south coast.

Leslie retained his love of aviation, even after his 'flying courtship' led to marriage with Stella in 1931 — a marriage which produced four children: Jill, Caroline, Georgina and Andrew Leslie. Accompanied by his friend Jim Proctor he made several flying trips to the continent. On one of these, a visit to North Africa, he was advised that it might be hazardous to fly across the Mediterranean. Rather than abandon the venture he contacted the Thomas Cook travel company which in turn contacted the Italian Air Force, which promptly despatched a seaplane to provide escort. In fact the seaplane proved so much the faster of the two planes that the pilot was forced to circle Leslie's aeroplane for the length of the journey. On arrival in North Africa Leslie's aeroplane was caught in a sandstorm, and

Leslie James Marr centre of photograph with his aeroplane.
To his left is Stella Cooper and a family friend, to the right is Jones the chauffeur.

Enjoying the trial run of the **Clevela** *in 1930 are left to right: Geoffrey Edwards Marr, Charles Towne, George Everingham, Edward Towne, Henry Atkinson and Percy Edwards.*

The new Marr trawler **Clevela** *dressed overall arrives at her home port of Fleetwood for the first time.*

the need to clean out the engine persuaded him to return home. The journey back to England went without incident but then darkness fell as the aeroplane approached Croydon Airfield. Unable to locate the runway Leslie set his aeroplane down deftly in a field full of cows and left it there while he and his friend located the nearest pub and enjoyed what he later described as 'A most magnificent steak'.

Such was the nature of the two young men who now set out to guide J. Marr & Son through the 'Thirties; a decade which opened promisingly enough. The winter of 1928-29 had seen an improvement in trade, prompting the Company to build two new 135ft home water trawlers — *Criscilla* FD23 and *Maretta* FD45 — at a cost of around £15,000 each. At the same time the old stalwart *Rattler* was sold. One of the original Marr fleet, *Rattler* had served the company for a remarkable 38 years; a span that had inevitably taken its toll. It is said that during her last survey Harry Ritchie, the Company's superintendent engineer, saw the Lloyd's surveyor checking the old trawler's plates with a chipping hammer and requested that he refrain from banging too hard for fear of going through. The surveyor responded by using his pencil to probe a weak spot — and to their mutual amazement it went through the plate! The tale probably owes more to exaggeration than fact, but it is a typical example of dockland humour.

The new vessels *Criscilla* and *Maretta* proved successful, and it was therefore decided to build four more. These — *Fyldea* FD72, *Clevela* FD94, *Armana* FD121 and *Cordela* FD120 — were all commissioned in 1930. Unfortunately the improved trading conditions were not maintained, and early in the 1930's the Fleetwood fishing industry felt the impact of the severe depression sweeping the world. Even the new trawlers began to make heavy losses, and the situation was becoming desperate. It was apparent that 135ft trawlers could not be profitably employed on the west coast hake fishery, but in contrast Hull's larger deep water trawlers were exploiting the rich fishing grounds off Bear Island, and the city was beginning to boom. Leslie Marr in particular began to feel that the Company should re-open in its original port.

The opportunity came in 1934 when the shares of an old-established Hull concern, the City Steam Fishing Company, were offered for sale. The whole of the capital was purchased by Marr, and the Company was back in Hull after an absence of 36 years. The manager of the City Steam Fishing Company, Fred Crawforth, was retained and became manager and head fish salesman for J. Marr & Son Ltd. in Hull — positions which he would continue to hold until 1939 when the coming of War forced the closure of the Hull business.

The four new trawlers were transferred to Hull to augment the two vessels of the City Steam Fishing Company — *Botanic* H463, and *Dairycoates* H270 — and in 1933 three former Hull trawlers — *Castlethorne* H427, and *Andradite* H176, and *Andalusite* H90 — were bought and transferred to Fleetwood as replacements. To further strengthen the Hull fleet two distant water trawlers were built: the *Westella* H124 in 1934, and the *Kirkella* H319 in 1936. These vessels cost £16,000 and £19,000 respectively, and were the first to be given the suffix '*ella*'. In 1935 the secondhand trawlers *Rhodelite* H5, *Ruby* H393 and *Zircon* H329 were purchased for the City Steam Fishing Company.

The fishing industry was not immune to the industrial unrest of the depression years; in March 1935 deckhands and cooks of the Hull fleet took strike action over the intention of the Hull fishing vessel owners to reduce liver oil money by 10 shillings per cask, at a time when fish prices were low. The dispute lasted three weeks, and during this time 246 trawlers remained tied up in the various docks.

By 1937 the rapid expansion of the Hull fishing industry brought its own problems. The market collapsed and the price of fish fell, with the effects being felt at all ports, particularly Fleetwood. This was despite the demise of the North Sea boxing fleet in 1936, when all 61 vessels were laid-up for sale. Fortunately the distant water trawler owners recognised the problem, and an 'economic investigation' research unit was established in an office on St. Andrew's Dock. This undoubtedly saved the industry. Prices were rationalised, uneconomic ships were laid-up, sold or scrapped, and fish landings at Hull, which had peaked at 6,568,938 cwts. in 1937 were reduced to 3,928,009 cwts. in 1939.

Although events in Hull tended to take the limelight the business there was essentially a branch, with the main operation remaining at Fleetwood. The directors continued to live there and to travel backwards and forwards between the two ports. The depression was producing a gradual decline in the number of trawler owners and vessels at Fleetwood; in 1929 the port had 178 trawlers registered by some 60 owners. Ten years later this had contracted to 112 trawlers owned by 21 companies. Marr's position at the port remained strong; with an average of 25 vessels the company held a major position in the Fleetwood fishing industry.

The Marr fleet had changed considerably over the years, through the buying and selling of ships and also as a result of losses at sea. In 1939 the fleet position was 21 vessels at Fleetwood and 8 vessels at Hull. The basis of the home water fleet was the 'Castle' type steam trawler of 125ft length, large numbers of which were built by the British Government between

The busy transport area of St. Andrew's Dock Hull in the 1930's.
During this era an average of 350 railway fish vans would leave the dock each working day in eight special express freight trains.

St. Andrew's Dock full of trawlers during the 1935 trawler crews' strike.

1916 and 1919. In 1939 the Company had 10 such vessels in its fleet.

With the worst of the depression now over the fishing industry was getting back on its feet again. Then, in September 1939, the Second World War broke out. Almost immediately two of Marr's vessels fell victim to the conflict when they were attacked by a submarine while fishing together at the Flannan Islands on the morning of 18th September. The *Arlita* FD188 and the *Lord Minto* FD51 were sunk by gunfire, the crews having first been transferred to the *Nancy Hague*, which was then ordered to return to Fleetwood at speed.

The incident seems almost symbolic in view of the fate which war was about to wreak on the fleet as a whole. Once again the Admiralty began to requisition trawlers — including those still under construction — for deployment as minesweepers, convoy escorts and anti-submarine vessels. Manned by R.N.R. fishermen they became part of the Royal Navy Patrol Service. Between the commencement of hostilities in 1939 and the evacuation from Dunkirk in 1940, the Company's entire fleet — with the exception of two small trawlers — was requisitioned for war service or was sunk.

Personal tragedy came hard on the heels of global disaster; on 24th October 1939 Edward Towne died suddenly at the age of 58, leaving a widow, Mrs. Annie Towne and a son, Charles. A man of sterling character, Edward Towne had served with the company for 37 years. Geoffrey and Leslie Marr had cause to be grateful for his good work, and for the support he provided when, as young men, they had found themselves running the business in most difficult times.

In November 1939 Fred Crawforth was appointed as a director of the City Steam Fishing Company, but sadly he too died suddenly just a year later. The management of J. Marr & Son was now solely in the hands of Geoffrey and Leslie, the two being assisted by Henry Atkinson. Henry had joined the company in 1913, been appointed secretary in 1929 and now, in 1940, was appointed a director.

Choosing to apply his flying skills on behalf of the War effort, Leslie joined the Air Transport Auxiliary. Among his tasks was that of ferrying aircraft from the factories to the front line air bases — an enterprise somewhat more perilous than his peacetime 'courtship' flying. Geoffrey remained in Fleetwood, and despite the pressure of operating the company alone, and running several trade organisations, he found time to join the Home Guard — where one of his companions on motorcycle duties was the show business personality George Formby.

At Hull the War led to a suspension of the fishing industry, and

*Edward Towne Secretary and Director of
J. Marr & Son Ltd.*

the Company's office on St. Andrew's Dock was closed. Later, during a heavy air raid in 1941, the premises were physically removed by a land mine which destroyed a large part of the northern end of the dock.

On 2nd June 1940 H.M.T. *Westella* was part of a group of three anti-submarine trawlers supporting the withdrawal from Dunkirk. Whilst attacking a contact the *Westella* and H.M.T. *Blackburn Rovers* entered a minefield and were sunk. The remaining vessel, H.M.T. *Saon*, picked up 36 survivors from the two stricken vessels. Other vessels from the Marr fleet which

*H.M.T. **Fyldea** served with the Royal Navy as a minesweeper during the 1939-1945 War.*

served at Dunkirk were *Jacinta* FD235, *Edwina* FD205 and *Velia* FD49.

As the War progressed Fleetwood became the country's major fishing port, thanks to its advantageous position on the west coast. As it had during the First World War, the Company launched into the agency business, handling countless Icelandic and Faroese vessels during the period of the conflict. The crews of these vessels were a boon to the local shopkeepers for they would fill up their holds for the journey home; packing them with everything from provisions to household goods — with pianos being particularly favoured. The Company also acted as agents and managers for a fleet of neutral vessels. In total J. Marr & Son handled, during the War years, £10,000,000 value of foreign fish landed at Fleetwood.

During October 1944 the first of the Company's requisitioned trawlers, *James Lay* LO333, was repatriated, and others were soon to follow. Accordingly Leslie Marr was released from the A.T.A. to help prepare for peacetime operations. It would be no easy task. During the course of the conflict the Company had lost 29 vessels, either while fishing or on active service, and to replace these had purchased 25 trawlers, mostly under requisition. When hostilities ceased, in the spring of 1945, the Marr fleet consisted of just six small trawlers.

Chapter 5:
THE POST-WAR REVIVAL

During 1945-46 surviving trawlers were returned from naval service to be re-converted for fishing operations. At Hull the vessels were registered under the ownership of the Hull Ice Company and managed by various owners. This gave all owners a financial share in the proceeds until they could purchase back the vessels to build up their fleets.

Following the cessation of hostilities it was realised that the coal burning trawler was coming to the end of its era. Oil fuel was more convenient and gave greater horsepower, and there was considerable encouragement to build faster ships that would use the low grade oil residues which were comparatively cheap.

The Company's first oil fired steam trawler was ordered on 15th June 1945 from the shipyard of Cook, Welton & Gemmell of Beverley, and was named *Southella*. At the same time two coal burning trawlers, on order from Cochrane's of Selby, were cancelled and two oil burners ordered in their place.

The Company's Hull branch re-opened on Monday 9th July 1945. Leslie Marr moved to Hull, accompanied by George Everingham who was appointed manager. Archie Bell was re-engaged as superintendent engineer and Robert Milns was engaged as fish salesman. Charles Holness was head of the shoregang.

On 14th January 1946 the *Marinda* FD155 was delivered, and was soon followed by other new vessels: *Josena* H207, *Navena* FD149, *Borella* H240, *Northella* H244 and *Southella* H303. To further strengthen the fleet the *Kirkella* H155 was purchased, and two other ex-naval trawlers which were renamed *Carella* H4 and *Westella* H349. By the end of 1946 J. Marr & Son were at the forefront in post-war fishing operations. The new and more modern trawlers were some three knots faster than pre-war vessels, and had more power for towing the trawl. The shrewd decision to order these vessels was now paying off; the order books of the shipyards were now full, and consequently the price of new vessels was increasing all the time. To consolidate its position the Company already had orders for new trawlers and was in a position to sell off the older ones at a premium. The *Northella*, for example, was sold in 1948 for £117,000.

To coincide with the delivery of the new trawlers key personnel were being released from their military service, and they were restored to their former posts within the Company. To further strengthen the Hull office, assistant superintendent Glen Riches and cashier James Doyle were transferred from Fleetwood. With the Company enjoying such a prominent role in the post-war fishing industry it was possible to recruit top class people to fill vacancies. The Company's list of top skippers included Leo Romyn D.S.C., Bill Drever, Charles Taylor, Jack Crewdsun, Bill Turner, George Clarkson, Charlie O'Neill, Steve Blackshaw, Tan Turner and Bill Harris.

Soon the volume of work being conducted at the Trident office was such that finding a working space was like engaging in a game of musical chairs, and it became necessary to acquire larger premises. Negotiations were opened to rebuild on the site of the old City Steam Fishing Company's office and the adjoining building. Contracts for the new premises were placed in 1946, and the new office of J. Marr & Son was opened in 1950.

One of J. Marr's greatest rivals was Boston Deep Sea Fisheries, but away from the fishing grounds there was often co-operation; in particular between Sir Basil Parkes and Leslie Marr, who ordered the first two oil burning deep sea trawlers for the British fleet: the *St. John* H254 and the *Southella* H303. This co-operation extended to having three motor trawlers built as a joint venture: the 136ft *Alan Water* H420 and *Thorina* H318, which were built at Beverley in 1946, and the 190ft *Lammermuir* H105 which was built at Aberdeen in 1950. These were very interesting vessels, being the first diesel trawlers of their type. Motor trawlers were not immediately successful as they lacked the torque of a steam engine and required 50% more power. Although the three trawlers were not a great commercial success they provided valuable information for the future.

After the War there was considerable uncertainty regarding the future direction of the home water side of the industry, and the four home water vessels delivered in 1946 — *Marinda*, *Navena*, *Josena* and *Thorina* — were all resold soon after entering service. Then, during 1947-48, the Company bought nine 'Castle' type trawlers as a stop-gap measure designed to maintain a reasonable sized fleet of trawlers at Fleetwood.

Tragically Bunt Harding, the superintendent engineer at Fleetwood, was killed in an accident while surveying a boiler on one of the Company's trawlers. His replacement was H.W.N. Mewse, known popularly as 'Jimmy', who was the son of one of the Company's top skippers, Jimmy Mewse.

During the War the Company had lost most of its key personnel to the armed forces, while over the same period a large volume of transactions had been undertaken for agency work. As a result the Company's account books were in a shambles and

*The **Kirkella** at Ellesmere Port in December 1945 being refitted as a trawler following her services with the Royal Navy during the 1939-1945 War.*

*Delivered in 1946 in the Company's new distinct livery, the fine looking **Northella** created great interest within the Hull fishing industry and a photograph of the vessel appeared on the front page of the "Hull Daily Mail".*

there was a clear need for someone with a good understanding of the fishing industry and with expertise in accountancy to resolve matters. So it was that in 1947 Harold Davison came to leave the Company's accountants Hodgson Harris to become the Company's secretary. Another prominent individual to join J. Marr from Hodgson Harris was Cliff Bennett, who later became secretary and a director.

In 1947, too, Dan Ellwood — who was assistant to Henry Atkinson at Fleetwood — was transferred to Hull and promoted to the post of office manager. Dan Ellwood was a man of outstanding character and ability, the perfect go-between to link senior staff and the owners. One of his tasks was to smooth out any problems that might arise when skippers came for their post-trip interview with either Geoffrey or Leslie Marr.

At Hull the fleet was constantly upgraded, with the older vessels being sold as new ones were delivered. The new arrivals during this period included the *Murella* H481 and *Junella* H497, built by Cochrane's at Selby, and the *Lorella* H455 built by Cook, Welton & Gemmell at Beverley.

Unlike their coal-burning predecessors the oil-fired steam trawlers required no tall funnel to keep smoke clear of the bridge, nor ash chutes to discharge ash over the side. This gave leeway for a certain amount of streamlining, and from 1948 there emerged the distinctive design featuring a short funnel incorporated into the bridge. The first of the Company's trawlers to boast this modern design were the *Cordella* H572 and *Thornella* H582, which were built by John Lewis Ltd. at Aberdeen in 1948. During the following year the same yard built the *Benella* H15 and the *Primella* H103. In 1949, too, three sister-ships, *Farnella* H41, *Starella* H75 and *Swanella* H42, were built by Cook, Welton & Gemmell at Beverley. The cost of building these vessels ranged from £70,930 in 1947 to £114,445 in 1949.

Archie Bell, the superintendent engineer, played a prominent role in the design of the trawlers built for the Company's Hull fleet. He had served his time with Amos & Smith and had the ability to produce fine drawings to convey the Company's requirements to the shipbuilder's design team. Archie Bell was a man of good presence, and one who commanded great respect.

The Company's involvement with the port of Hull was steadily increasing. By now Leslie Marr had established a family home at Swanland, and in 1949 Geoffrey Marr came to the city with his family and took up residence in Elloughton. Thus the Marr family came to be re-established in Hull after an absence of half a century.

As is frequently the case with twin brothers the two men shared a particularly close bond, and this was apparent in their working relationship. Although they might disagree over certain points of policy they never fell out, and they became renowned throughout the fishing industry for the high standards they set and the progressive outlook they displayed. Among their achievements was the building of the first successful diesel trawlers and the development of the stern trawler, and they pioneered the freezing of fish at sea.

During the late 1940's Geoffrey's teenage son Geoffrey Alan gained his first experience of the business when he made his first fishing trip in the *Swanella*, with skipper Leo Romyn. As events turned out he discovered as much about the Cold War as about fishing, for the trawler was arrested by a Russian patrol vessel and held for questioning inside the Kola Inlet, on the Murmansk coast, for five days before being released.

Around this time, too, Leslie Marr undertook another of his celebrated air trips. His original intention was simply to visit South Africa in a bid to sell some of the company's older trawlers, but being unable to obtain a flight he bought a single-engined Proctor aircraft, an aircraft without even a radio, and, accompanied by his former wartime C/O Joe Shoesmith, flew to South Africa under his own power; a journey of about 14 days. During this and future visits Leslie established a good rapport with the local fishing community; in particular with the National Trawling & Fishing Company of Cape Town, which subsequently bought the trawlers *Iolite* H372, *Bulby* FD147, *Marinda* FD155, and *Borella* H240. Later Geoffrey Alan was able to take advantage of this good relationship, visiting South Africa to spend seven months working with the National Trawling & Fishing Company — and an evening at Cape Town's celebrated Kelvin Grove Club celebrating his 21st birthday!

Around this time the Company added a further element to its operations. Since the War most trawler repairs in Hull had been undertaken by Humber St. Andrew's Engineering Company Ltd., which had been formed in 1946 by the merging of two old-established ship repair companies: Humber Shipwright Co. Ltd. and the St. Andrew's Engineering and Shipwright Co. Ltd.. All the local trawler owners had bought shares in the merged company, according to the number of vessels they owned, with J. Marr & Son Ltd. owning 10% of the share capital.

The restoration of the port's fishing fleet brought an increase in the demand for repairs; an increase which exceeded Humber St. Andrew's capabilities and resulted in delayed sailings as vessels awaited repair. To avoid this, and all the disruption that went with 'missing the tide', Marr's began to employ the Globe Boiler & Ship Repair Co. Ltd. to undertake some of its repair work. By 1949 it had become apparent that ownership of its own ship repair

*The **Thornella** H84 laid up for survey and repairs by the Globe Boiler & Ship Repair Co. Ltd. in the 1960's. The photograph was taken from the Company's office window.*

facility would be in the Company's best interests, and accordingly Globe was acquired.

Globe was in a somewhat run-down state, with its plant in poor condition, but it had a top class foreman heading each of its shops: Fred Allen in the boilermakers shop, Joe Gledhill in the shipwright's shop, Stuart Swan in the fitters shop and Harry Spink in the blacksmiths shop. It was Marr's intention to make a substantial financial investment in the company, and accordingly Dan Ellwood was appointed a director and Dick Sumners moved from Fleetwood to become the manager. Dick was not an engineer but he soon gained respect throughout the company for his ability to bring out the best in people and pour oil on troubled waters.

The acquisition and restoration of Globe was a significant project but it seems modest in scale compared to the operation which the Company was engaged in at the same time but on the other side of the world. During 1948 Leslie Marr and Harold Davison had visited Hull's Royal Station Hotel to meet with Harry Leggeburke, Mark Buxton, a Mr. McNichol and — principally — Alfred Francis Philip James. The last mentioned, an Australian who had served in the R.A.F. during the War, had read about a pre-War Australian fishing venture while working for the magazine *Picture Post* — and he convinced everyone at the meeting that this was a project worth pursuing.

The Company decided to invest £10,000 in the venture, and sold to the Anglo-Australian Fisheries Company two trawlers which were past their useful life for fishing out of Britain: the *Ben Dearg* FD286 and the *Commiles* FD285. Despatched under the command of two Merchant Navy captains, and with crews recruited from Scotland and prepared for a long absence from home, the vessels spent two months sailing half-way round the world to their new base, the port of Albany. Their safe arrival was a tribute to the seamanship of those aboard.

The chief skipper on the Australian operation was Alf Britton, and Billy Richardson was the superintendent engineer. Mr. Howlett, one of the shareholders, went to Albany to run the office, with Alfred James. The Western Australian Government supported the initiative enthusiastically, and over the course of three years made a major financial investment in the project. There certainly proved to be large shoals of marketable fish in the Southern Australian Bight, but there were also large quantities of sponges which tended to clog the nets. The ice plant also proved to be inadequate but what really defeated the project was the geography of the fish markets; Perth was 300 miles away and transport costs swallowed almost all the profit from each catch. Eventually it became apparent that the conception of the project was flawed and that massive losses would ensure if it were continued. So, in 1952, Leslie Marr and Harold Davison flew out to Australia and persuaded Alfred James to close down the Anglo-Australian Fisheries Company.

Although Marr's made no profit from the Australian venture it sustained no real financial loss, and those involved in the project thoroughly enjoyed the experience; especially the novelty of working with a variety of colourful Australian characters over the course of three years. The two old trawlers were perhaps the main losers from the project; they ended their years providing target practice for the Royal Australian Navy.

Between 1949 and 1950 orders were placed for six new diesel engine home water trawlers, four of which were to be built at Beverley and two at Selby. These were the prototypes of the modern home water trawlers which would prove outstandingly successful in future years. Each vessel cost around £73,000 and this had to be raised without Government assistance despite the fact that the Sea Fisheries Act, which contained provision for grants and loans, was being drafted at the time. However the Company's reward was to be several years ahead of its rivals, and the project gave a new lease of life to the Fleetwood branch, which had been rather in the doldrums for some time. From 1950 the post-war revival of Fleetwood's fishing industry began gathering pace.

Jimmy Mewse, the superintendent engineer, must take full credit for the development of the diesel engines used to power the motor trawlers. While serving with the prestigious Blue Funnel Line, of Liverpool, he had gained certificates of proficiency in both steam and diesel, and the latter was invaluable to the Company in the development of the motor trawler fleet. The main engines were supplied by Mirrlees, which usually built generating engines; its introduction to the manufacture of marine engines was through J. Marr & Son and Boston Deep Sea Fisheries. It was Jimmy Mewse who made it possible to adapt the engines for use at sea; spending a tremendous amount of time developing lubricants and bearings to help produce the required torque and power.

View of St. Andrew's Dock, circa 1954 taken from the Company's boardroom window.

*The **Westella** and **Andradite** at the North End, Fleetwood circa 1949.*

*The new diesel trawlers fitting out at
Princes Dock Hull in the early 1950s.*

*Mrs. Mackenzie launches the
Starella H75 at the shipyard of Cook
Welton & Gemmell on 30th March 1949.*

Chapter 6:
THE 'FIFTIES AND THE COMING OF THE COD WARS

The 'Fifties began with a change of lifestyle for Geoffrey Alan Marr, for he joined the Army to do his National Service and was based on the Isle of Wight. During his time in uniform he obtained the qualification of Marine Navigator Class 3, which would later become useful when running the Company's trawlers.

The number of these continued to increase. In 1951 the first of the 190ft. three-deck bridge trawlers was delivered by Cook, Welton & Gemmell of Beverley, at a cost of £129,000. She was named *Northella* H159 and grossing 787 tons she dwarfed most existing trawlers. The following year two sister trawlers — *Lancella* H290 and *Kirkella* H209 were delivered. The two had the advantage of a 15 knot maximum speed, which was 2.5 knots faster than any other trawlers of the time. They were thus able to fish longer than other vessels yet still arrive in Hull ahead of their rivals and secure a better position on the fish auction market.

The first of the new diesel vessels, the *Hildina* H222, was also completed in 1952, and operated out of Hull for a while. The others — *Velia* FD116, *Idena* FD136, *Irvana* FD152, *Gavina* FD167 and *Luneda* FD175 followed in rapid succession, and all were based at Fleetwood. Tragically, on 1st December 1953, *Hildina* sank while fishing off the Orkneys. Eight survivors were rescued by *Velia* but six crewmen were lost including skipper George Clarkson D.S.C.

Unfortunately a depression now hit the fishing industry, and prices plunged until trawler fleets were barely covering their running costs and fish merchants were struggling to make a profit. The situation caused deep concern at all levels, and the Government set up the White Fish Authority to re-organise, develop and regulate the British white fish industry.

On 15th May 1952 the Icelandic Government added to the industry's problems by declaring a four mile fishing limit, measured from the headlands. Prior to this, Iceland's fishing limits and territorial waters had been three miles measured from the low tide level mark; a limit accepted by most countries and dating from the era when three miles was the maximum range of a cannon. The change excluded all vessels — including Iceland's own — from 5,000 square miles of first class grounds, which the Icelandic Government claimed were being over-fished. The

British fishing industry responded by banning Icelandic trawlers from landing their catches at British ports, but lengthy negotiations ensued and in 1956 a compromise was reached. Although Britain did not recognise the four mile limit it was agreed that there would be no fishing in that area, and once again Icelandic trawlers were permitted to land at British ports.

In 1953 the Company's first deepwater diesel trawler *Brucella* was delivered from Cook, Welton & Gemmell of Beverley at a cost of £155,000. A prototype of the large traditional diesel trawler, the *Brucella* H291 was highly successful and very popular with crews.

On 26th January 1955 the whole nation was stunned by the news of the loss of *Lorella* H455 and *Roderigo* H135 with all 40 crewmen during severe weather near Iceland. The two trawlers were top class vessels but stood no chance against the freak conditions of heavy seas and freezing winds. The whole city went into mourning, but from the tragedy there later emerged one good outcome for it led to the establishment, on 18th November 1956, of the Hull Fishermen's Trust Fund. The Trust was created to provide a fund for the relief of fishermen disabled in the course of their duties, and also for the relief of the widows and other dependents of fishermen who perished at sea.

In 1955 the *Kirkella*, with skipper Charles Taylor, won the Silver Cod Trophy; the prestigious award presented by the British Trawlers Federation to the skipper and crew of the trawler which landed the largest weight of fish in a calendar year. the *Kirkella* gained the trophy by landing 46,589 kits of fish, valued at £129,563, from 339 days at sea.

Then in the following year it was the turn of the *Lancella*, with skipper Bill Turner, to secure the trophy by landing 45,936 kits of fish, valued at £131,633, from 340 days at sea. Six of the top fifteen trawlers in the competition belonged to J. Marr & Son Ltd., including the top earner *Thornella* H84 which grossed £144,442. In 1957 a ceremony was held at the Fish Mongers Hall, at which the 1955 and 1956 Silver Cod trophy winners were jointly presented with their awards by His Royal Highness Prince Philip.

In 1956 Geoffrey Alan Marr was appointed a director of the Company, and became joint manager at Fleetwood with Henry Atkinson. Around this time the Government's Grant and Loan scheme for the building of middle water trawlers ushered in a twenty year period of prosperity for the Fleetwood fishing industry. All Fleetwood's trawler owners took full advantage of the scheme, which allowed the building of trawlers up to a maximum of 139ft. Although intended largely for middle water fishing these vessels were permitted to make two trips a year to

St. Andrew's Dock Hull
facing east towards J. Marr & Son Ltd.'s Hull offices, circa 1954.

*The spectacular side launch of the **Collena** FD20 at the shipyard of Cochrane's of Selby in 1955.*

The hulls of trawlers built at Beverley were towed down the river Hull to be fitted out with engines and winches at the premises of C. D. Holmes of Princes Dock, Hull. The journey down the river usually took three high tides. The trawlers had to be moored until sufficient water was available to move further down the river.

Skipper Bill Turner receiving the Silver Cod Trophy from His Royal Highness The Prince Philip in 1957.

distant water grounds, but little advantage was taken of this concession owing to the cost of changing from middle to distant water fishing gear. Under the scheme the Company built the *Collena* FD20, *Dorinda* FD22 and *Jacinta* FD21 in 1955 at Selby, and *Lucida* FD437, *Josena* FD150 and *Edwina* FD162 in 1957-58 at Beverley.

During 1957 the Company took delivery of the *Swanella* H141 from Cook, Welton & Gemmell of Beverley. This was the last steam trawler ordered for the fleet. Two years later the *Corena* FD173 built at Selby, was the first to have a variable pitch propeller. This was built by Escher Wyss, of Ravensbruck, a company which had previously built variable pitch turbines for the water industry. Wishing to establish itself in the marine world the company approached J. Marr & Son Ltd., and *Corena* became the recipient of their expertise. Unfortunately many problems were encountered with the variable pitch propeller, as it was not compatible with side fishing trawler operations. Later, however, it was fitted to stern trawlers with no problems at all.

Meanwhile Marr's on-shore operations continued to progress, and in 1957 the Company acquired the old-established fish importing and exporting business of Andrew Johnson Knudtzon Ltd. With the purchase came a 6,000 ton capacity public cold store — one of the largest in the north of England — which Andrew Johnson Knudtzon had erected to handle the catches from its venture into deep freezing fish at sea. Tom Summers, who was secretary of the Active Fish Company, became manager of the new acquisition, and was later appointed a director.

By now J. Marr & Son Ltd. had become a major undertaking, and was recognised as the largest privately-owned business in the British fish trade. Geoffrey and Leslie Marr's main ambition had been to establish a network of companies involved in all aspects of the fish trade: from catching and landing to marketing, processing and transporting to the buyer. This ambition had been achieved so comprehensively that the Company even owned fish & chip shops which it leased-out.

During 1958 Geoffrey Alan Marr transferred to Hull, and Mark Hamer was appointed assistant manager at Fleetwood. At the same time Mr. A. T. J. Hogan was appointed superintendent engineer at Hull.

On 23rd June 1958 the Prime Minister of Iceland issued a decree which extended Icelandic fishing limits to 12 miles. The extension was to come into effect from 1st September, and it led to the first of the acrimonious disputes between Britain and Iceland which would come to be known as the Cod Wars. It

The premises of Andrew Johnson Knudtzon Ltd. in Hull.

The interior of Andrew Johnson Knudtzon's cold store in the 1960's.

became necessary for trawlers fishing between the four and the twelve mile limits to do so in 'boxes', under the protection of the Royal Navy. Despite harassment by Icelandic gunboats trawlers from Hull, Grimsby and Fleetwood continued to pursue their task doggedly, and the amount of fish caught remained constant.

The following year J. Marr & Son's fleet became the first at Fleetwood to consist solely of diesel engined vessels. During that year, too, the Dinas company of Fleetwood was purchased, and along with the trawlers came some highly successful skippers. In the spring of 1959 the *Gavina* FD167 with skipper Sid Christy, fished at Iceland with spectacular results, averaging £248 per day from July to December. The other five early-1950's diesel trawlers were despatched to Iceland and proved similarly successful, emerging among the port's top earners with skippers Victor Buchini jnr., W. F. Wright, T. Christy, G. Beech, H. Daniel, J. Bruce, Billy Taylor, Albert Crewdson and G. Beech jnr..

By the end of 1959 the last of the Company's old coal burners had been sold, and shortly afterwards the last of the deep water motor side-fishing trawlers were ordered from Cook, Welton and Gemmell of Beverley. The sister ships *Benella* H132, *Northella* H98 and *Westella* H194 were powerful and handsome vessels, and were regarded as the finest sidewinders ever built. The smaller *Starella* H219, built for fishing at Iceland, would be delivered in 1960 and have the distinction of being the last side-fishing trawler ordered for the Company's Hull fleet.

As the 'Fifties drew to a close the controversy between Britain and Iceland over fishing limits continued unabated, but for Geoffrey Alan Marr the decade ended with personal celebration for he married Margaret Rose Elisabeth Stirk; a union that would produce four children: Charles Roger, James Geoffrey, Sophie Ann Sarah and Catherine Elizabeth Joanne.

*The **Starella** H219 the last deep water side fishing trawler built for the Company.*
She was highly successful out of both Hull and Fleetwood.

Chapter 7:
THE 'SIXTIES: THE ERA OF THE FREEZER TRAWLERS

In 1960 Harold Davison, who had been company secretary since September 1947, was appointed a director. A great enthusiast for the 'freezing at sea' project, Harold was closely involved in all the experimental work leading up to the building of the new trawler *Junella* H347. Later he was involved with the research into the thawing, storage and marketing of the fish, making a major contribution to the Company's success in this field.

In that year too Marr built a new near water trawler, the 115ft. *Lavinda* FD159 for fishing in the Irish Sea and Scottish grounds. This gave the Company three spheres of operation at Fleetwood: distant, middle and near water. During 1961-62 two new 140ft. middle water trawlers, the *Arlanda* FD206 and *Armana* FD207 were added to the fleet.

Other companies watched with interest but could not send their 'Grant and Loan' vessels to Iceland for more than two trips as this was classed as distant water. Eventually the White Fish Authority came under increasing pressure over this ban, and in 1962 the restriction was withdrawn, allowing 'Grant and Loan' trawlers to fish wherever their owners chose.

In 1961 the *Northella* H98 skippered by Charles Drever, won the Silver Cod Trophy with 41,176 kits of fish valued at £162,062 from 312 days at sea. Charles Drever's father, Bill, came third in the *Westella* H195 with 37,117 kits of fish valued at £163,177. The Company's fleet of fifteen trawlers also had the distinction of being the highest average earners at the port of Hull.

On 28th February 1961 the long-running dispute with Iceland over fishing limits was finally brought to a conclusion, with Britain agreeing to accept the twelve mile limit. The British fishing industry greeted this decision with anger and dismay, and it was generally felt that the Government had been forced into this compromise by diplomatic pressure from America, Russia and Norway. Norway itself now extended its fishing limits to 12 miles, although British trawlers were granted a concession allowing them to fish to within six miles of the coast for 10 years. A similar concession had been granted by Iceland but for a duration of only three years, and dissatisfaction with this — plus indignation over provocative landings of Iceland-caught fish at Hull — led to the Trawler Officers Guild calling an abortive protest strike. A year later, on 12th March 1962, the Russian Government introduced its own 12 mile fishing limit.

Amidst all this J. Marr & Son continued to make progress in a project which had been initiated in 1958 to establish a practical system for freezing fish at sea. The experiments were prompted by the fact that fish stored in crushed melting ice become inedible after about fifteen days, which limited the time trawlers could spend at sea; often forcing them to return home partly full to avoid landing poor quality fish.

Initially a pilot freezer plant was stowed under the whaleback of the *Marbella* H52, then later a small freezing compartment and a low temperature store was built into the hold of the *Junella* H399. Andrew Leslie Marr accompanied skipper Syd Marvel on the *Junella* to gain an insight into these experiments, during which the first few days' catch of some 3,000 stones was successfully frozen, and the remainder of the hold then filled in the traditional manner.

The four years of tests conducted by the Company came to fruition in March 1962 with the launching of the *Junella* H347 at the shipyard of Hall Russell at Aberdeen. The vessel was 240ft. long, grossed 1435 tons and cost £350,000 to build — £50,000 of this being provided as a special grant from the White Fish Authority. The first vessel of its type in the world to freeze its entire catch, the *Junella* had the ability to handle 25 tonnes of fish a day in her newly designed vertical plate freezers. There were, in addition, facilities for blast freezing large fish such as Halibut, and storage capacity for up to 300 tonnes. Commanded by skipper Charles Drever the vessel proved so successful that a further nine freezer stern trawlers were built for the Company's Hull fleet between 1964 and 1975.

To process the frozen fish a new purpose-built factory was constructed in Walcott Street, Hull, and a new company — Junella Foods Limited — was formed to market the product. It was found to be impossible to thaw large quantities of frozen fish simply by playing water over them and accordingly Harold Davison designed and patented a thawing machine specially for the task. This was installed in a building opposite the cold store and defrosted the fish very successfully.

During 1961 a series of exploratory voyages were conducted to the Anton Dohrn Bank off the east coast of Greenland; the *Brucella* H291 and Boyd Line's *Arctic Ranger* H155 working in conjunction with the British research vessel *Ernest Holt*. Andrew Leslie Marr sailed with the *Brucella* to gain experience in the Company's operations, and around the same time Geoffrey Alan Marr sailed with the *Junella* on her first voyage to Greenland. It seems fitting that the two great grandsons of William Marr should visit the very waters that had claimed the life of their seagoing

*The **Junella** H399 landing both fresh and frozen fish at Hull during the experiments into freezing fish at sea.*

*The freezer stern trawler **Junella** H347 arrives at her home port of Hull on 11th July 1962.*

ancestor — and particularly appropriate that they should complete the circle of history at such an important time for the Company.

Despite an increase in the basic rates of pay the fishing industry had begun to experience crew recruitment problems at all major fishing ports. In order to maintain a high calibre of personnel most companies transferred whole crews to new vessels and disposed of the older, less profitable ships.

In 1961 J. Marr & Son owned 31 trawlers: 14 at Hull and 17 at Fleetwood. Between 1962 and 1966 the Company disposed of seven steam trawlers from the Hull fleet: the *Swanella* H141 in 1962, *Kirkella* H209 in 1963, *Cordella* H572, *Marbella* H52 and *Southella* H303 in 1965, *Bayella* H72 and *Farnella* H399 in 1966. They were replaced by the new freezer trawlers: *Junella* H347 in 1962, *Northella* H301 in 1964, *Kirkella* H367 in 1965, *Marbella* H384 in 1966 and *Swanella* H421 in 1967.

In October 1962 the Company concluded the purchase of the fish processing and distribution company Jackson Mills Ltd. Founded by 'Mick' Jackson and Sam Mills in the late 1940's this enterprise had flourished impressively until by 1975 it was the largest transport company in Hull. Jackson Mills' extensive distribution network included depots in locations ranging from Newcastle, Middlesbrough and Liverpool to Southampton, Portsmouth and Exeter, and it was the Company's proud boast that it could deliver fish for any of its markets by 6.0 a.m. the day after landing. At its peak the Company's distribution arm, Jackson Mills Transport, owned 135 vehicles and 50 trailers. Some 40 lorries were based at Hull, with 90 smaller vehicles deployed at the depots. For return loads the company arranged to pick up Guernsey tomatoes and Fyfes bananas at Southampton Docks, and vegetables from the Vale of Evesham, and deliver these to Hull's Humber Street market.

The acquisition was the result of close co-operation between the two companies over the previous six years — Jackson Mills vehicle fleet had long been serviced by the Flyover service station, another of J. Marr's companies. In acquiring the company J. Marr gained Jackson Mills' modern fish processing factory in Gillett Street, and the transport fleet which operated from a garage in Parrot Street.

On 20th January 1963 Leslie James Marr died, at the age of 59. He had served as a director for 38 years and had made a major contribution to the re-establishment of the Company at

*Frozen fish landed from the **Junella** being loaded onto one of Jackson Mills' lorries to be transported to the Cold Stores on 29th August 1962.*

Senior staff with Harry Atkinson in 1965.
Back row left to right: Harold Davison, Dan Ellwood, Mark Hamer, Cliff Bennett,
Percy Edwards (uncle of Geoffrey Marr).
Front row left to right: Andrew Marr, Harry Atkinson, Geoffrey Marr and Alan Marr.

Hull in the early post-war years. He was also the instigator of Marr's impressive post-war shipbuilding programme — from the post-war years to the freezer era of the 1960's — and beyond the confines of the Company had become a prominent and well-respected member of the fishing community.

On 19th February 1963 Andrew Leslie Marr was appointed a director of the Company.

As the 'Sixties progressed Marr's freezer fleet continued to expand. On 15th September 1964 the freezer stern trawler *Northella* H301 was delivered by the Aberdeen shipyard of Hall Russell Ltd. At 245ft. length and 1718 tons she was the biggest trawler in the British fishing fleet, and was purchased at a cost of £484,000. It would prove to be money well spent, for a year later the *Northella* would land a British record catch of 507 tonnes of codstuffs. In 1965, too, the freezer trawler *Kirkella* H367 was delivered, again by Hall Russell, and on her second voyage established a new national record of 550 tonnes from a 39 day trip. *Marbella* H384, built by the Goole Shipbuilding & Repair Company, was delivered on 21st April 1966 and also set up a new

record of 613 tonnes. *Swanella* H421, also from Goole, arrived on 31st January 1967 and yet again set up a new record with a catch of 665.5 tonnes. All of these records were set up by skipper Charles Drever, who was in command of each vessel when it was new. Then on 6th February 1969 the *Southella* H40 was delivered by Hall Russell, its length of 246ft. and breadth of 41.8ft. making it the largest British trawler. In 1971, under the command of Alfred Eagle, she would become the top British freezer trawler with a catch of 2,547 tonnes from 335 days at sea.

These successes prompted other trawler owners to place orders for this type of vessel, and by 1969 22 freezer trawlers were operating out of Hull, six of these being owned by Marr. In January 1964 the Company placed orders with C. D. Holmes of Beverley for two *Arlanda*-type trawlers, the *Maretta* FD245 and the *Zonia* FD236. Built at a cost of £169,000 these were the last two side-fishing trawlers built for the Company's Fleetwood fleet.

In September 1965 Henry Atkinson retired from the Company, and in October Mark Stanley Hamer — who had been assistant manager at Fleetwood since 1958 — was appointed a director of the Company and manager of the Fleetwood trawling business.

In the following year Fleetwood's only freezer trawler, the *Criscilla* FD261, was built by Hall Russell. The vessel was 185ft in length with a gross weight of 952 tons, and was specially designed to operate from Fleetwood; she was compatible with the port's crane system for unloading, and her beam and draught were exactly suited to the lock width and sill depth.

In 1967 the White Fish Authority chartered the *Kirkella* for an exploratory fishing trip to south-west Africa. Skippered by Charles Drever, and with Geoffrey Alan Marr aboard, the vessel left Hull on 18th October and steamed approximately 12,000 miles before returning to Hull on 16th December. Her catch comprised 100 tonnes of frozen fillets including hake, king klip, bream, snoek and horse mackerel which could be assessed for commercial values and retention of quality after freezing.

The winter of 1968 brought a sequence of disasters that stunned the whole country and severely damaged the morale of Hull's trawlermen. In January the *St. Romanus* and *Kingston Peridot* sank with all hands during severe weather, and on 4th February the *Ross Cleveland* was also lost. In all 58 crewmen perished and only one was saved. The tragedy left the fishing community in a state of shock, and public outcry led to the *Orsino* being chartered by the Board of Trade to act as a 'Mother Ship' and assist trawlers fishing at Iceland during the winter months. Also the former Swedish auxiliary sailing ship *Miranda* was acquired by the Board of Trade and converted into a 'Mother ship'.

Despite being marred by this historic disaster the 'sixties were a good decade for the Hull wet fish fleet, and one which saw many vessels produce impressive performances. In 1968 the *Primella*, with skipper Bill Wilson, won the Silver Cod with a landing of 40,844 kits of fish valued at £181,761 from 348 days at sea. The *Primella* H98 had previously won the trophy in 1961 when she was known as the *Northella* — a name transferred to the new freezer trawler in 1964. The *Primella*'s 1968 achievement was the last of its kind, for after that year the Silver Cod Challenge Competition was replaced by the Distant Water Challenge Shield.

In 1968 the Company extended its operations into Aberdeen, acquiring the whole of the capital of Peter & J. Johnstone Limited, an old-established company of trawler owners and fish salesmen with branches in Fraserburgh and Macduff. The fleet acquired included *Glenstraun, Loch Kildonan, Forward Grace, Forward Pride, Jacamar, Radiation, Paramount* and *Partisan*.

The Fleetwood trawlers *Gavina* FD167 and *Idena* FD136 had been transferred to Aberdeen in 1967 to strengthen this fleet.

In January 1969 Andrew Leslie Marr married Else Lica Andersen. They now have four children: Alexander, Christian, Sebastian and Natasha.

Just a month later, on 20th February 1969, Geoffrey Edwards Marr died, at the age of 64. He had been a director of J. Marr & Son for 44 years, and chairman for 40 of those. During this span he guided the Company successfully through the slump of the 1930's and the devastation of the Second World War; challenges which caused the demise of many other fishing companies. By acquiring ancillary companies and developing the fishing fleet Geoffrey Edwards and his twin brother Leslie James had made J. Marr & Son the largest privately owned fishing company in Britain. Geoffrey Edwards was also a major figure in a number of trade associations including the Hull Fishing Vessel Owners Association, the Fleetwood Fishing Vessel Owners Association, the British Shipping Federation, British Trawlers Reinsurance Association and the Fleetwood Trawlers Mutual Insurance Company.

On 11th March 1969 Geoffrey Alan Marr succeeded his father as chairman.

Chapter 8:
THE 'SEVENTIES AND THE END OF AN ERA

The 'Sixties closed with the resignation of Mark Hamer as manager at Fleetwood, and the appointment of Jim Cross in his place. At the same time Jim Hind, who for six years had served as wireless operator with Sid Christy in Fleetwood's top trawler *Maretta*, came ashore and was appointed assistant manager.

During the early 'Seventies the new chairman demonstrated the Company's faith in the future of the distant water fishing industry by embarking on a multi-million pound shipbuilding programme. Between 1970 and 1976 a total of 21 vessels were built, ranging from 106ft. 114 ton wet fish trawlers to 230ft. 1469 ton freezers. The Company collaborated closely with the builders to incorporate new and revolutionary design features in eight classes of new stern trawler.

Eleven wet fish trawlers, in four classes, were built for Fleetwood. These were: the 153ft. Class: *Gavina* FD126 (1971), *Luneda* FD134 (1971) and *Irvana* FD141 (1972). In the 166ft. Class: *Jacinta* FD159 (1972), and *Fyldea* FD182 (1973). All of these were built by Clelands Shipbuilding Company at Wallsend, except for *Irvana* which was built by Grangemouth Dockyard Ltd. The 120ft. Class — *Collena* FD221 and *Velia* FD220 — were built in 1973 by Richard Dunstan Ltd. at Hessle. The 128ft. Class — *Norina* FD324 (1975) and *Idena* FD325 (1976 — were built by the Goole Shipbuilding and Repair Company. The 129ft. Class — *Armana* FD322 and *Navena* FD323 — were built in 1976: the former by the Drypool Engineering & Dry Dock Co. Ltd. at Hull, the latter by Beverley Shipbuilding & Engineering Co. Ltd.

Four freezer stern trawlers, in two classes, were built for Hull. These were: *Farnella* H135 (1972), *Cordella* H177 (1973), *Northella* H206 (2) (1973) and *Junella* H249 (1975). All four were built by the Clelands Shipbuilding Company, which was part of the Swan Hunter Small Ships Division.

Six wet fish stern trawlers, in two classes, were built for Aberdeen. These were, in the 106ft. Class, *Glen Affric* A175 and *Glen Esk* A184, built in 1971 by J. Lewis & Son Ltd. at Aberdeen. And in the 117ft. Class: the *Glen Moriston* A238 (1973) and

Landing at Fleetwood are three of the new highly successful wet fish stern trawlers.
*Left to right: **Navena** FD323, **Jacinta** FD159 and **Armana** FD322.*

*Being prepared for her next trip **Farnella** H135 is moored on the "dry side" of St. Andrew's Dock, a few months before the dock closed in 1975.*

Glen Coe A283 (1973) and *Glen Urquhart* A364 (1974) built by the Goole Shipbuilding and Repair Company.

The wet fish stern trawler *Gavina* was the first of the new trawlers to be delivered, arriving in May 1971. During her first year, under skippers V. Buccini and G. Wignall, she grossed an impressive £244,638 from 17 trips.

From 1970 onwards fish prices rose substantially; soaring by a record 45% in 1973 alone. In the first year of the decade 120,589 tons realised £16,246,527 at Hull, but only six years later a mere 62,557 tons realised no less than £36,613,216. At fishing ports throughout Britain top skippers vied with each other so fiercely that records were broken almost every month — but rising running costs blunted the impact of these impressive returns. Only a few top vessels were making a profit, and most of the British fleet were barely breaking even.

In 1972 J. Marr engaged in a joint venture with the Vesty Family, having been approached to put two freezer trawlers into their company: (United International) Amalgamated Trawlers of Haute Bay, near Cape Town. The Company was familiar with the area, having deployed the *Kirkella* there on a research programme, and the project seemed an ideal way of diversifying its activities there. Accordingly the *Junella* and the *Northella* were despatched to Cape Town, having been renamed *Yellowfin* and *Bluefin*.

Regrettably the two vessels proved somewhat advanced for the recipients, who were unfamiliar with diesel-electric, and it was necessary to send people down to assist periodically. Two who worked particularly hard to keep the vessels operating were Jack Knaggs of Knaggs Electrical, who had formerly served with Broady's, and Bob Gledhill, who had been the assistant superintendent at Hull.

Around this time the Company was hit by the effects of the Middle-East oil crisis, which sent oil prices soaring. At this time, too, the fishing grounds were being subjected to very heavy fishing, so fish prices were extremely low and the size of the fish very small. The fish was marketed through the Vesty company, and large stocks of fish were held; these being paid for by the trawling company, which was known as Atlantic Trawling. Eventually funds were exhausted and it proved necessary to dispose of the company. Some of the vessels were purchased by a company known as Sea Harvest, while the two freezer trawlers were sold to Peter Kuttell, whose company Kuttell Fish operated out of Cape Town. In all Geoffrey Alan Marr made eleven trips to Cape Town in one year to complete the arrangements, and a successful conclusion was reached only after Chris Unis, the Minister of Finance at Cape Town, granted a loan of one million

rand to enable Peter Kuttell to purchase the two freezer trawlers, thereby enabling J. Marr to leave South Africa without any debts. The venture cost the Company two vessels and a considerable amount of money, but at another time, under different circumstances, it could well have proved successful.

On 1st September 1972 the Icelandic government unilaterally declared a 50 mile fishing limit; a move rejected by the European fishing nations. Once again the British fleet had to fish in 'boxes' under the protection of the Royal Navy. Despite these limitations, and harassment by Icelandic gunboats, fishing continued successfully. Then, in October 1972, the new limit was officially recognised. Access within the new zone was strictly limited, and close seasons and conservation areas were established.

In that year the Company diversified into a new field of operations: the provision of 'standby vessels'. Following the discovery of gas and oil in the North Sea during the mid-1960's this industry had expanded rapidly. This in turn had brought an increasing need for safety vessels to be on stand-by at the rigs to carry out evacuation if the need arose. Trawlers were ideal for this role, and many moved over to stand-by work as fishing opportunities declined.

Marr's involvement in these activities stemmed from a fortuitous meeting at an old boys' reunion at Stowe School between Andrew Marr, who was manager at that time, and Bruce Claridge, now operating Colne Shipping at Lowestoft. Colne was already undertaking stand-by work but lacked the larger vessels required to cover the fields north of the North Sea and Shetlands. Marr had just introduced the *Gavina* class of trawlers at Fleetwood, and was finding difficulty in manning the *Josena* class. These contrasting problems were resolved to the mutual benefit of the two companies; Marr initially secured stand-by work for the *Josena* FD150 and *Edwina* FD162, under arrangements with Colne, and by 1982 fourteen of the Company's vessels were occupied on stand-by work.

The growth in this area of activities led to the development of J. Marr & Son's offshore operations. Jim Hind devoted much time and effort in this field and it was largely through his endeavours that the Company became a major force in offshore activities. Having moved to Hull in 1982, Jim Hind became the Company's commercial director in 1987.

The rising cost of fuel oil during the 1970's brought about the premature demise of the steam trawler fleet. A steam trawler required an average of twelve tons of heavy oil per day, and by 1974 the cost per ton had risen to £33 — with a further increase to around £50 per ton expected. This, combined with other running costs, almost eliminated the chance of a profitable trip, and accordingly the Company's last two steamers — the *Thornella* H84 and *Lancella* H290 — were sold for scrap during 1974. In that year Britain's top wet fish trawler was the 15-year old *Westella* H194, with skipper Bob Warren, which grossed £453,475 for fifteen trips and spent 338 days at sea.

In June 1975 the *Jacinta* FD159, under skipper Bill Taylor, made history with the largest ever landing by a Fleetwood-based trawler. The catch, comprising 3,008 kits of fish taken during only 19 days at sea, sold for £35,282.

That year also saw the delivery of *Junella* H294, the last wholefish freezer stern trawler to be built for British owners. Despite restrictive quotas requiring catches to be one-third each of cod, haddock and mixed with White Sea species, *Junella* had a successful maiden voyage, thanks to the combined skills of skipper Alfred Eagle and chief engineer Don Jarrett. The 60 day trip produced a catch of 620 tonnes of fish.

1975 also saw the ending of an era with the closure of St. Andrew's Dock, which had been the home of the Hull fishing industry since 1883. The fleet and fish merchants now moved to new purpose-built premises at Albert Dock.

Then, in October 1975, the Icelandic Government inflicted a major blow on the fishing industry by unilaterally declaring a 200 mile fishing limit. The move sparked a year of hostilities during which the British fleet continued to operate in the forbidden zone, protected by warships of the Royal Navy from the harassment of Icelandic gunboats. Civilian vessels were also chartered to hinder the gunboats' attempts to cut the fleet's trawl warps, including some Hull-based ocean-going tugs and the Marr freezer trawler *Southella* H40, under the command of skipper Ches Abbot.

Despite every effort it proved impossible to achieve a compromise in the dispute, and on Wednesday 1st December 1976 — perhaps the blackest day in the history of the British fishing industry — the 200 mile limit was recognised and British trawlers were effectively barred from the Icelandic grounds. Canada, Norway and Russia had already established their own restrictions in response to concern over the exploitation of their territorial waters by an increasingly large international fleet of modern, sophisticated trawlers, and thus the British deep sea fishing fleet was now excluded from the greater part of its traditional grounds.

The impact was devastating; almost all of the prominent trawler

*During the 1975-1976 "Cod War" the British frigate H.M.S. **Galatea** keeps a watchful eye on the Icelandic gunboat **Odinn**.*

The deep water fleet laid up at Albert Dock, Hull in 1978. These large highly sophisticated trawlers
had few places that they could fish, their activities being severely affected by strict fishing quotas and limited seasonal access.

owners gradually sold their vessels and left the industry. Many of these were companies whose histories stretched back to the days of the sailing smacks and whose ships and men were well-known at every major port. Now they passed into the pages of the history books. For J. Marr & Son, however, 1976 heralded the end of an era rather than the end of the Company. Survival depended upon diversification, and the Company therefore applied its skills and resources to two new areas of operation: home water fishing and stand-by and survey work.

On 17th April 1977 Henry 'Harry' Atkinson died. His efforts on behalf of J. Marr & Son had helped to make it Fleetwood's principal fishing company. He was a member of the council of Royal National Mission to Deep Sea Fishermen, and in 1965 he had been awarded the O.B.E. in recognition of his services to the fishing industry.

Chapter 9:
THE NEW ERA: FISHING OPERATIONS

With the loss of the Icelandic fishing ground the Company's Fleetwood vessels had to turn to the home water grounds. The 'pair fishing' method was considered and then developed quite successfully after observation of Spanish fishing vessels which had followed this practice for many years. The method was particularly effective for catching cod, especially on the fine grounds of Muckle Flugga and the Patches.

In Hull the distant water trawler owners turned their attention to mackerel; a species prolific around England's south-west coast and the west coast of Scotland — the Minches in particular. The trawlers' owners won the right to undertake trawl fishing inside the Minches; a court decision not favoured by the Scottish pelagic fishermen.

Initially mackerel was caught for reduction into fish protein but to avoid the damage to stocks that would result from heavy fishing it was subsequently decided to freeze the mackerel and supply it to markets already established in West Africa. Accordingly a new company — J. Marr (Seafoods) Ltd. — was formed to buy mackerel from UK trawlers and export it to West Africa, an operation which proved sufficiently successful to gain the Company the Queen's Award for Export in 1980.

J. Marr (Seafoods) Ltd. went on to trade fish throughout the world, using a barter system. This involved arranging for Eastern bloc factory ships to process the catches of the Scottish and Irish pelagic fishing fleets. The architect of this successful operation was Roger Johnson, who was closely supported by Andrew Marr.

Eventually the Ministry of Agriculture, Fisheries & Food placed catch uptake restrictions on the distant water freezer trawler fleet, making it impossible to operate a viable fishery from this stock. This was a sad time for this section of the industry, which could only suffer while watching Dutch freezer trawler operators go on to build a successful fleet of modern freezer trawlers to feed a Government-supported export market. By now, however, the Scottish pelagic fleet was operating with ever-increasing success, and fortunately the Company was engaged in marketing a large proportion of their fish.

During the late 1970's French trawlers from Lorient and Concarneau were catching substantial quantities of white fish on the westerly grounds of the British Isles and landing at Fleetwood.

It was decided to develop a fishery along the lines of the French operations, and to this end Jim Cross the general manager of Fleetwood operations went to Brittany and recruited two French skippers.

In 1977 Charles Roger Marr joined the Company and was based at Fleetwood. Following the family tradition he spent the next three years at sea. During this time he observed pair fishing, pelagic fishing with trawl and purse and traditional demersal fishing. In 1982 he married Bridget Robson, and they have three children; Annabelle, Philip and Polly.

By the late 1970's the distant water fishing industry was in a poor state; at all major fishing ports the rusting hulks of laid-up trawlers littered the docks. Worst hit by the stringent quotas and high running costs were the side fishing trawlers; every month trawlers which were once household names were towed away to the scrapyard. At Hull vessels which had once proudly gained the Silver Cod Trophy lay side-by-side on the mud of the Victoria Dock slipway, awaiting the cutter's torch. Of the Company's four remaining Hull side fishing trawlers, the *Brucella* H291 and *Primella* H98 were scrapped in 1977-78, a buyer was found for *Westella* H194, and *Benella* H132 eventually went for survey work.

Around this period the Company moved its Aberdeen fleet to Grimsby, in a bid to keep these vessels working the North Sea fishing grounds. Unfortunately the financial results were poor and Andrew Marr spent a considerable amount of time and effort selling this fleet to foreign owners.

With numerous vessels being made redundant many top skippers were available, and it was during this time that Ken Grubb and Dave Wright were attracted to Fleetwood to command two of the Company's vessels. These two skippers brought with them considerable experience of fishing in the North Sea, particularly for coley.

Market trends were by now dictating where vessels landed, so Hull and Grimsby became more prominent in this procedure. In July 1982 the decision was taken to transfer the Company's eight wet fish stern trawlers to Hull, in a last-ditch attempt to maintain a fishing fleet. The search for new markets was now on, and during the winter, one of the trawlers became the first Marr vessel to land in Germany — a development that marked the beginning of a new trend of foreign landings. As a result of this trend the grossings increased, and this gave the fishing side of the Company a much needed boost.

The remaining freezer trawlers at Hull were doing their best to eke out a living from mackerel fishing and small quotas of white fish when, in 1982, the Falklands War began. Five Hull freezer

*The "**Cordella** Group" passing under the railway bridge across the Firth of Forth*
whilst returning home from the Falklands to Rosyth, in October 1982.
Whilst the five trawlers were in Naval Service the M.O.D. paid wages to all the crews of these ships who were unemployed.

stern trawlers — *Cordella*, *Farnella*, *Junella*, *Northella* and *Pict* — were called in to Rosyth Dockyard for conversion to undertake minesweeping duties. Crewed by officers and ratings of the Royal Navy these vessels went on to give sterling service in the South Atlantic before being returned to their owners in October 1982. The charter of Marr trawlers for minesweeping duties dates back to 1976-77, when the concept of using stern trawlers for pair sweeping operations was pursued; the Ministry of Defence chartered trawlers and their crews to train R.N.R. personnel in the use of this type of vessel.

In 1983, to help reduce the size of the British fishing fleet, the Government introduced the decommissioning scheme, following agreement on the Common Fisheries Policy in Brussels. Those owners who were not already in the hands of the banks took the opportunity to leave the industry for the payment of £400 per gross ton. The balance of the Hull freezer fleet was decommissioned and converted for survey work, and three former Fleetwood trawlers — *Gavina* FD126, *Irvana* FD141 and *Luneda* FD134 — were sold to CAM Shipping for offshore work. J. Marr & Son decommissioned six of its trawlers as part of the scheme, but the sum received was taxed by the Inland Revenue and the amount returned only after an appeal before the Tax Commissioners and a lapse of several years. It was a sad decline for the once powerful distant water industry which, in its heyday, had fulfilled 90% of the country's fish requirements.

Of the eleven freezers of the Marr fleet, four were sold to foreign companies for fishing. These were *Junella* H347, *Junella* H294, *Cordella* H177 and *Northella* H301. Two others, the *Swanella* H421 and *Kirkella* H367, were sold for stand-by work. The *Criscilla* FD261 was sold to R.A.E., and the *Farnella* H135, *Marbella* H384, *Northella* H206 and *Southella* H40, were retained by the Company for use outside the fishing industry.

On 27th January 1984, the Company suffered the loss of the *Navena* FD323, following an ingress of sea water into the factory deck. All the crew were safely rescued by helicopter, the *Navena* was subsequently beached at Scarborough where she capsized.

By 1985 the Company was down to just five fresh fish trawlers. During this year fishing operations continued their positive trend and the *Armana* FD322, with skipper Malcolm Trott, was the first white fish trawler to gross over £1,000,000 in a calendar year. Fishing only in home waters the *Armana* landed a total of 30,059 kits from 22 trips during which she spent 320 days at sea. Her nomadic existence is illustrated by the ports of landing; nine at Bremerhaven and Cuxhaven in Germany, six at Aberdeen, three at Fleetwood, two at Birkenhead and two at Hull.

Further improvements in 1986 led to the purchase, from Claridge Trawlers Ltd. of Lowestoft, of the 39.7 metre wet fish stern trawler *St. Patrick*. The vessel was renamed *Gavina* H24 and based at Hull.

On 30th December 1986 a £5 million order was placed with Cochrane Shipbuilders of Selby for two new 38.5 metre long wet fish stern trawlers, to be named *Thornella* H96 and *Lancella* H98. These were the first deep sea fishing trawlers to be built for the company in twelve years. The first to be completed, *Thornella*, was launched by Mrs. Bridget Marr, wife of Mr. Charles Marr.

The launch of the *Thornella* was an emotional moment as only a few years earlier in the midst of the fishing depression it appeared that no new ships would ever be built again for the Company's fishing operations. The *Lancella* was launched on 18th April 1988, both trawlers entering service in that year.

In the summer of 1988 Nigel Atkins joined the Company as a director. Mr. Atkins brought with him valuable knowledge of quotas and EC regulations, the complexities of which had become an incredible burden to carry.

In 1988 the purse-seiner *Glen Helen* FD220, which had been acquired for pelagic fishing, was put up for sale as the Company wished to return to freezing-at-sea for pelagic species. To this end, in April 1988, the Company's first pelagic freezer trawler was bought from Holland. The *Voorwaarts*, which had been built in 1975, was renamed *Swanella* H142. During the initial stages of the operation the Company employed a Dutch fishing master, who was able to bring considerable knowledge to the Hull skipper and his crew. Then, on 24th February 1989 a further pelagic freezer trawler, the *King Jupiter*, was purchased. This former Dutch trawler, built in 1974, was renamed *Marbella* H99.

On 26th January 1990 the *Lancella*, with skipper Dave Wright, achieved a British record cash sale from a single landing, grossing £260,324 from a 16-day trip to the Norwegian coast. This record was broken in February 1991 by *Jacinta* FD159, with skipper Dennis Beaumont, which grossed £270,516 for a 20-day trip to the Norwegian coast. These figures are fascinating when compared with those of the *Northella* H98 which in 1961 had grossed £162,062 for the full year.

In May 1990 the beam trawler *Petronella* H171 was acquired. This Dutch-built trawler was purchased to catch North Sea plaice and Dover sole — one of the few sectors in which the fishing quota was not being completely filled. Unfortunately within two years the quota available for Dover sole was so small that the vessel became uneconomic, and so it was sold.

By the early 1990's it was recognised that the Hull fish processors were in desperate need of an all-year-round supply for their network of customers. In August, with this in mind, the

*At the launch of the **Thornella** H96 are left to right:*
Mrs. Alan Marr, Mrs. Robson mother of Gordon Robson,
Alan Marr, Bridget Marr wife of Charles Marr, Charles Marr.
In the front – Jannie Marr and behind her Mrs. Robson and, at extreme right, Gordon Robson.

Company purchased the freezer stern trawler *Myre Fisk 1* from Norwegian owners and renamed her *Southella*. Built in Norway in 1986, this 51 metre vessel can freeze up to 50 tonnes of fish per day, and can carry 400 tonnes of frozen fish in block form. Under the command of Marr's senior skipper, Ken Grubb, the *Southella* H240 has become one of the UK's most successful trawlers.

In April 1994 this trend was to continue when the Company added the former Icelandic freezer stern trawler *Gudmunda Torfadottir* to its fleet. Built in Norway in 1989 this 53.1 metre vessel was given a total refit on arrival in Hull, and the temporary name *Irvana*. Command was given to Ken Grubb, who moved from *Southella* with most of his crew — a common practice that keeps a highly skilled team together and also gives younger skippers and crews the opportunity to move up to better vessels. After a highly successful maiden voyage to Bear Island the new trawler was given the name *Swanella* H1065, the fifth Marr trawler to bear this name.

To make way for the new trawler the eighteen year old *Armana* was sold to a trawler owner in the Irish Republic.

At the present time the Company operates eight trawlers fishing in distant and home waters.

Chapter 10:
THE DEVELOPMENT OF J. MARR SHIPPING LIMITED

During the early 1970s a number of the Fleetwood and Aberdeen side trawlers became uneconomic in their existing designed roles. They had effectively been replaced by the modern stern trawler fleet coming on line at both of these ports.

The old saying goes "as one door closes another one opens" and the North Sea oil fields were coming on stream. The oil and gas platforms, located in a hostile marine environment, were manned by large numbers of personnel who needed an effective rescue procedure in the event of a disaster.

The side trawler lent itself ideally to be converted to standby rescue vessels and many of the Marr side trawlers were transferred to this role.

James Hind, the Assistant Manager of the Fleetwood office, undertook specific responsibility for this new sphere of business.

Jim had great foresight and it wasn't long before he realised there were other business opportunities for the hard pressed fishing fleet.

During 1976 Hunting Survey required a suitable vessel for oil exploration work in the North Shetland and Norwegian Sea area. The *Criscilla*, no longer able to fish at Iceland, was proposed as suitable for this role and proved to be so during an initial five month charter period. Following this successful charter the Company decided to undertake a full conversion of the vessel for this new activity. A twelve month charter was agreed with Sonamarine, the sub-sea exploration arm of British Petroleum, with modification of the vessel being undertaken by the Globe Boiler and Ship Repairing Company. Skipper Roy Hadgraft was appointed senior captain, with John Cannan as his chief officer and relieving master.

During 1978 Marr took over the management of the *Aqua Star*, a survey vessel owned by Fairfield Aquatronics; a subsidiary of a major American shipping group headed by Laszlo Karoly. During 1980-81 Marr were successful in gaining the management of two further vessels for Fairfield: *British Viscount* and *British Vanguard*. At this time Marr also purchased *British Viking*,

Swanella

Pacific Horizon.

which became the *Swanella*, and ultimately the *Sir Walter Raleigh*.

1979 saw the completion of discussions with Horizon Exploration, a leading Seismographic Survey Company, which had a long term requirement for two vessels. In January the research vessel *Subsea I* was acquired and converted at Hull by Globe Engineering. The vessel was renamed *Pacific Horizon* and she still remains an active member of the Shipping fleet to this day. The second vessel *Marbella*, was also converted to a deep seismic survey vessel at Smiths Dock Company at Middlesbrough. She was renamed *Northern Horizon* and served with distinction in her new role.

Starella.

During 1979-80 the *Southella* undertook a one year charter as a fishery protection vessel for the Scottish Office.

In July the *Criscilla* was sold to the Royal Aircraft Establishment, a transaction which resulted in the purchase of a replacement survey vessel, *Subsea 2*, which was renamed *Starella*.

The Company's foothold in Seismic work was further consolidated in 1981 when the *Southella* was converted by the Humber Graving Dock and Engineering Co. Ltd. and renamed *Seisella* for her long term charterers Seismographic Services Ltd. As a native Yorkshireman, Seismographic's senior director, Jack Smith, was delighted to be associated with a Yorkshire company.

The clouds of war gathered once again for the Company when in April 1982 all four of the remaining large stern trawlers — *Junella, Farnella, Cordella* and *Northella* — were requisitioned by H.M. Government for the Royal Navy. As the "*Cordella* Group" they served as minesweepers during the Falklands War. This prompted the Company's considerable interest in the Falklands, and in 1983 the fishery research vessel *G. A. Reay* was purchased from the Ministry of Agriculture, Fisheries and Food to investigate the possibility of establishing a fishery in the Falkland Islands. Visits to Japan by James Hind and Richard Lander in 1985 led to discussions with Mr. Matsutomi of the Kanega (KSJ) Association. As a result the KSJ commenced fishing around the Falklands with, at one time, a fleet of over forty vessels.

Farnella returned in the Autumn of 1982 and was chartered by the Indian Government for scientific survey work. During this period the vessel completed a 75,000 mile voyage dredging mineral-rich nodules from deep areas of the Indian Ocean.

In October 1983 the *Northella* began what was to be a long-term association with the M.o.D (N) as a naval navigation training vessel. The Captain was Jim Rimmer of Poulton le Fylde, and after his retirement he was followed by Tony Barkworth and Rick Tobin. The senior naval officers aboard were Lt. Commander David Graham and Lt. Commander Doug Sewell.

At this time *Cordella* was undertaking duties as a guardship for Trinity House in the Straits of Dover, whilst a major electric power line was being installed for CEGB and EDF (France). During 1984, however, the vessel was sold to Skeggs Seafoods of Nelson, New Zealand and left Hull on 1st December under the command of Skipper Barkworth.

Following her return from India, *Farnella* was chartered by the United States Department of the Interior for survey work off the Pacific coast, its task being to locate mineral deposits and earthquake faults. During the 21,500 mile voyage the vessel performed so successfully that the Americans chartered her for a much larger task.

United States Department of the Interior
GEOLOGICAL SURVEY
RESTON, VA. 22092

In Reply Refer To:
Mail Stop 915

August 27, 1985

Mr. Alan Marr
J. Marr and Son, Ltd.
St. Andrews Dock
Hull, England HU3 4PN

Dear Alan:

On behalf of the U.S. Geological Survey, I would like to commend the exemplary job by J. Marr and Son during the last 2 years of the GLORIA program. From personal participation and observations during my on-site visits to England, personal visits with your staff in the United States, and from all of the reports of our Survey personnel returning from cruises or visits to England, morale and a sense of cooperation, enthusiasm, and accomplishment have been extremely high throughout our effort to date. While this sustained high level can be explained in part by the exciting nature of the scientific work, a large amount of credit must be given to the smoothness with which the entire field program has been executed and to the teamwork that characterizes this program.

I would like to particularly commend Jim Hind and his staff for their vital role in making this large-scale field operation the remarkable success that it has been in 1984 and 1985. Jim has fostered constructive interaction between all parties involved in the field operations and in negotiations leading up to these field efforts, responded positively to suggestions of our scientists, and has directed the operations in a most successful manner. Jim's outstanding management, knowledge of requirements pertinent to our science efforts, and positive "can-do" attitude is crucial for the procurement of a long-awaited set of seafloor imagery in the Exclusive Economic Zone of the United States. It is a credit to Jim that his staff reflects all his fine qualities which has resulted in a unique group of outstanding engineers and ship's crew. You have every reason to be extremely proud of these professionals. We extend to them our sincere appreciation for their efforts. A special thanks to Anna Kalnaj. She has been an absolute pleasure to work with, and her efforts on our behalf are greatly appreciated. We will miss her, but wish her the very best.

The surveys in the Gulf of Mexico are proceeding on schedule despite Hurricane Danny. We look forward to the port stop in New Orleans as Department of the Interior Assistant Secretary Robert Broadbent and USGS Associate Director Doyle Frederick will tour the FARNELLA and hold a news conference on September 4, 1985. I'm personally excited about my first cruise on the FARNELLA during the last 2 weeks of October.

It is a continuing pleasure to work with your organization on this exciting program. I look forward to seeing you again, my best to your family.

Sincerely yours,

Gary W. Hill, Ph.D.
Manager, Offshore Geology Program
Associate Chief, Office of Energy
and Marine Geology

Letter from United States Department of the Interior.

On 18th December 1984 an agreement was signed by the British Institute of Oceanographic Sciences and the United State Geological Survey to survey and map more than five million square miles of the seabed in America's 200 mile exclusive economic zone, using the first GLORIA: Geological Long Range Inclined Asdic. Such was the importance of the work that the I.O.S. provided *Farnella* with the brand new GLORIA Mk II, designed to map the seabed. The survey job took seven years to complete and the *Farnella* travelled the equivalent of eight times round the world. The fact that she never missed a single day's work in all that period is a tribute to the crew and the shore-based back-up team. Among the visitors to the *Farnella* during her long tour of duty was President Reagan's long-time associate Bill Clark, Secretary of the Interior — the U.S.G.S. being a prominent section of his department. On 1st September 1992 the *Farnella* returned home to the port of Hull and a hero's welcome. Crowds of people lined the quayside and the vessel and her crew were officially welcomed home by the Lord Mayor of Kingston upon Hull and Admiral of the Humber, Councillor Dennis Barber. Those who commanded the *Farnella* during her American enterprise included Roy Hadgraft, John Cannan, Mike Patterson and John Nichol, and today the vessel's seven year task is recognised as one of the greatest scientific sea ventures of all time.

Since 1985 J. Marr Shipping has managed and maintained the weather ship *Cumulus* for the Meteorological Office. For several years the *Starella*, purchased in 1980, worked in tandem with the *Cumulus*, with the U.K. Met. Office being responsible for the former and the Netherlands Met. Office for the latter. However, with the decision by the Netherlands authority to discontinue their sea observation programme, the *Cumulus* was sold for the princely sum of £1 to the United Kingdom Met. Office. The handover ceremony was held at Hull and attended by Government Ministers from both countries, senior members of their respective Meteorological Offices, the Lord Mayor of Kingston-upon-Hull, and the Company Chairman Geoffrey Alan Marr.

During 1986 Marr Technical Services Ltd., commonly known as MTS was registered as part of the restructuring then taking place. It was intended to develop MTS as a consultancy arm of the Shipping Division, to provide technical services to internal Marr companies, and also to external clients. Marr had by that time built up a significant expertise in Survey Ships and other specialist technologies, and MTS would market these.

The Company commenced formal trading in September 1987, with the first contracts being the design work associated with the conversion of the ex-*Junella* to the *Hill Cove* for the Falklands and the refit of *Pacific Horizon* with a totally new 3D seismic system.

The Company next led the combined J. Marr team on the Single Role Minehunter Trials Ship, where MTS were responsible for the tender preparation, the design work and project management on the conversion of *Northern Horizon* for a successful 2 year contract with the M.o.D.

In the early days, services were provided to a host of clients, and support given to MVML during tendering, mobilisation and demobilising from charters. Newbuilt small craft were designed and several refits conducted, giving a constant and hectic workload.

The specialist experience in Survey and Research ships led to the Company being retained by several shipbuilders around the globe for assistance in specifying, designing and building these modern and complex ships. St. Johns Shipbuilding in Canada, Swan Hunter on Tyneside, Mjellem & Karlsen in Bergen, Ching Fu Shipbuilders in Taiwan and Transfield in Melbourne appear in the list of clients.

In addition to helping shipbuilders, MTS has also been deeply involved in the mobilisation and support of programmes with research establishments. The Company was actively involved in managing the mobilisation of the US-sponsored project to find the sunken German Battleship *Bismark*.

An ongoing relationship has developed with scientific bodies in Korea, and this has led to involvement in a host of projects, including charters for Antarctic operations, design assistance on newbuild research ships, and the procurement of special equipment. This procurement role led the Company into the unique contract of delivering a refurbished "Stalwart" amphibious vehicle to the Korean Antarctic Base, with the contract giving the MTS Naval Architects the somewhat unusual task of "inclining a lorry". It also led to a further unique record for the Company when the vehicle was delivered to the Antarctic by "launching" it down the stern ramp of MVML's *Falklands Right*.

The scope of Technical Services offered has increased over the years, with the office now providing the Information Technology support to the Shipping Division as well as Health & Safety for the Group. The traditional facilities of Naval Architecture, Design and Draughting have all been maintained. Fisheries Consultancy has recently been added to the range.

The Company is also responsible for maintaining the Group's interests in Research & Development and has actively participated in several teamings and consortia for the development of new marine technologies.

The expansion into Fisheries Consultancy has been supported by active investment around the globe, and MTS personnel have been deployed to various overseas locations to obtain first-hand insight and information on local requirements. The Marr experience in Catching, Marketing, Research and Patrol are all proving to be valuable assets.

The wide breadth of knowledge and experience within the Marr establishment led to MTS being retained by the UK Government Foreign and Commonwealth Office to provide Know How support to the Government of Lithuania. This has in turn led to further ongoing contracts and involvement in the restructuring of the entire Lithuanian Deep Sea Fishing Fleet. The original single Company "JURA" possessed a vast fleet supported by an exhaustive establishment and infrastructure, all greater than required in the modern fishing industry. MTS is helping to rationalise this towards a profitable and secure industry.

A very important area of operation for J. Marr Shipping has been the supply and operation of vessels for fishery protection duties. One notable contract was the charter, management and eventual sale of the *Criscilla*, originally the fishery protection vessel *Jura*. She operated successfully in Mauritanian waters in conjunction with the German concern GTZ. The charter was so successful that the Charterers exercised their option to purchase and *Criscilla* was renamed *N'Madi*. To date she continues her role patrolling the Exclusive Economic Zone of Mauritania.

Since 1987 J. Marr Shipping has provided vessels and crews for the Falkland Islands Patrol Service, which is responsible for protecting one of the most valuable resources of the Falkland Islands — its fishery. To protect this the Falkland Islands Government exercises an interim fishery control zone extending to 150 miles from a central point. British and foreign vessels are licensed to fish within this circle, and the area is policed by patrol vessels and spotter planes. The vessels provided by J. Marr Shipping are: *Falklands Desire* (*Seisella*) 1986-1989 and 1992-1993, *Falklands Right* (*G. A. Reay*) 1987, *Falklands Right* (*Lancella*) 1988-1990, *Falklands Protector* (*Eastella* and *G. A. Reay*) 1990-1993, *Cordella* 1992 to the present.

Having developed considerable operational experience in fishery protection work the Company is now well positioned to take advantage of the expected increase in the Global requirement for improved fisheries management.

Recent success has come from securing a few months charter with the British Indian Ocean Territories Administration for fisheries patrol work around Diego Garcia. For this task the *Northern Horizon* underwent minor conversion work in Singapore prior to departure.

In a fascinating departure from the norm, in 1989 J. Marr Shipping chartered the vessel *Star Hercules* to play a major role in the JASON project; one of the most dramatic undersea search operations of this century. During the previous year Dr. Bob Ballard — of *TITANIC* fame — aboard the *Starella*, had searched in vain for the wreck of the German battleship *Bismark*, which had been sunk by units of the Royal Navy on 27th May 1941. On 28th May 1989, with time for only twelve days on site. Dr. Ballard began his search for the wreck once more, working from *Star Hercules* and using the underwater search robot "ARGO". On 8th June the wreck was finally discovered and excellent quality film footage and photographs were obtained.

During 1989 James Hind had been studying the dynamic positioning market. He felt it would be an important sector in which to be established and so, in 1990, the *Northern Horizon* was converted into a dynamic positioning vessel by a team of craftsmen and technicians headed by Joe Watson, technical director of J. Marr Shipping. The D.P. conversion enables the vessel to hold a position above a pipeline so that surveys and repair work can be conducted by remote operated vehicles, which are controlled from the D.P. vessel.

Northern Horizon was successfully placed on the huge Zeepipe contract. This involved the laying of a sub-sea pipeline from Norway to Belgium. *Northern Horizon*'s task, equipped with Remotely Operated Vehicles, was to ensure the pipe had been positioned correctly and safely.

J. Marr Shipping, eager to expand their management expertise further afield, keenly contested the management tender for the two Scottish fishery research vessels *Scotia* and *Clupea*, a contract they subsequently won. This contract was again retained after the initial three year period following the re-tendering exercise during 1994.

During 1992 the Skeggs Group of New Zealand informed J. Marr Shipping that it was prepared to sell the trawler *Cordella* which it had bought in 1983. The Company repurchased the vessel with the intention of using her as a research and patrol vessel in the South Atlantic. After a refit the vessel was despatched to the Falkland Islands, where she is in service at the present time. The *Cordella* replaced the *Falklands Protector*, formerly the *G. A. Reay*. The *Falklands Protector* proceeded to South Africa where she was ultimately sold in 1993 to Aquanymphe of Cape Town.

Following the success of the *Northern Horizon* it was decided to convert the *Farnella* to a D.P. vessel. On 22nd February 1994, following a £2-million refit, the *Farnella* was renamed *Northern Prince* and returned to sea on charter to the Anglo-Dutch company Fugro-McClelland.

Over the past 20 years J. Marr Shipping Ltd. has consolidated its expertise in vessel management and is now well established and respected in its field. The Company presently operates seven of its own vessels and managed three Government owned research vessels.

Chapter 11:

STELLARIS BUSINESS TRAVEL AND
OTHER DEVELOPMENTS

By 1984 both J. Marr Shipping and Marr Seafoods were truly international companies with a growing need to transport personnel to all corners of the world. Because the volume of travel was becoming so great the decision was taken for the Company to establish its own business travel agency. This led to the founding of Stellaris Business Travel and two travel consultants Mike Bedford and Ian White were recruited from local travel agent Matador Travel to head-up the new operation.

Although the Marr Group travel requirement was substantial it was not long before other major companies in the City moved their travel accounts to Stellaris and the Company enjoyed steady growth from the early days of its inception.

During 1987 Stellaris moved from Princes Dock Side to the Marr Building on St. Andrew's Dock, having outgrown its original offices and in 1992 established a further branch at York. The most experienced business travel consultants in the York and Leeds areas were recruited headed by David Jopling ensuring the branch's successful development.

A policy of offering experience and efficient business travel services has continued to attract major client companies in the Humberside and Yorkshire region and to further consolidate Stellaris's position a third branch is to be opened on South Humberside during 1995.

Mrs. Richard Weeks (Katherine Elizabeth Joanne Marr) daughter of Mr. G. A. Marr is currently a member of the staff of Stellaris Business travel.

The opening of Stellaris Business Travel on St. Andrew's Dock in 1987
by the Lord Mayor of Hull, Mrs. Marjorie Smelt.
Left to right: James Marr, Mrs. A. Smelt the Lord Mayor, and Geoffrey Alan Marr.

*The construction of the "Marysol" commercial centre
at Sologrande in Southern Spain.*

OTHER DEVELOPMENTS

In April 1986 the Group broadened its commercial interests in the leisure industry sector, which was demonstrating strong growth potential at that time. A Spanish hotel project and commercial property development was purchased from an English hotel group, Poste Hotels.

Located in Southern Andalucia, near Gibraltar, the hotel principally served the golfing market and as such attracted a number of prominent international companies sponsoring corporate hospitality.

In 1989 the construction of the 4000 sq.m. "Marysol" commercial centre was completed. Its attractive Moorish design aroused considerable interest from many local businesses and by the middle of 1990 the majority of the offices and shops had been sold.

Following a period of very difficult trading from the hotel operation, the Group eventually sold its interests in June 1992, to a local Spanish hotelier.

In 1988 J. Marr Ltd. made an offer to third party shareholders in the Fylde Ice and Cold Storage Co. Ltd. to purchase their shares. This was successful and J. Marr Ltd., has now a controlling interest in this Company which it has been associated with since 1908. Fylde Ice has its headquarters at Fleetwood. The present managing director John Kelly succeeded Tony Long who successfully piloted the Company through the very difficult years of the 1980's when the fishing industry was going through its severe restructuring. The Fylde Ice and Cold Storage Co. Ltd. is now the leading producer of packed ice used in domestic and catering application. This makes a very useful addition to the Company's traditional cold storage and ice making facilities.

During 1986 the Company's profile was changed by a de-merger which was approved by an extraordinary General Meeting of shareholders on 30th April 1986. J. Marr & Son Limited was restructured into two companies and its assets were shared between Mr. Geoffrey Alan Marr's family and Mr. Andrew Leslie Marr's family. On 6th January 1987, Andrew Marr resigned from the Company and formed a new business — Andrew Marr International Limited — which incorporated the fish processing, fish selling, fish trading and cold storage businesses. Geoffrey Alan Marr retained the interest in trawling, shipping and engineering businesses.

ANDREW MARR INTERNATIONAL

Andrew Marr International Limited was formed on 18th April 1986. just before the de-merger, to take over the shareholdings in certain subsidiaries of J. Marr and Son Limited.

The initial companies forming the new Andrew Marr International Group were:

J. Marr (Seafoods) Limited	— International fish Trading
Marr Frozen Foods Limited	— Fresh and frozen fish processing
J. Marr (Aberdeen) Limited (including Peter & J. Johnstone Ltd.)	— Fish selling and fishing vessel management
Andrew Johnson Knudtzon Limited	— Cold storage
Stellaris Business Travel Limited	— Travel agents

Shortly after the merger, it was agreed that Andrew Marr International would move out of the old offices on St. Andrew's Dock and subsequently new offices were built at Livingstone Road, Hessle, which were completed in 1989.

Following the de-merger, Mr. Andrew L. Marr became Chairman and Mr. Dennis W. Chapman was appointed Financial Director. The Board was strengthened when Mrs. Else Lica Marr was appointed a Director in June 1987. Frank Dee was appointed Managing Director in February 1989, bringing with him considerable commercial experience from outside the fishing industry.

Frank Dee resigned as Managing Director in January 1992, to resume a career in food retailing and Roger Johnson was appointed in his place. On the retirement of Dennis Chapman in October 1989, Mr. A. Michael Smith was appointed Financial Director.

During the first five years several important changes in the structure of the new Group took place.

Stellaris Business Travel Limited was sold back to J. Marr Ltd. to add to their other leisure and travel interests.

Marr Frozen Foods Limited was sold to its Management in April 1989, although Andrew Marr International retained a 10% interest for a further four years.

Andrew Marr International acquired Stanleys Toffee Limited in April 1990, a new venture completely outside the fish related activities of the Group. Stanleys specialised in the manufacture of personalised confectionery products for the gift and leisure market and it was further strengthened in July 1990 by the acquisition of Border Country Cousins.

The Peterhead Ice Company, which is one of the largest ice manufacturing businesses in the UK, was acquired in November 1991.

A major refurbishment took place at Andrew Johnston Knudtzon Cold Stores in the early nineties incorporating a move into more specialised storage facilities and in 1994 the business was greatly strengthened by the acquisition of Polar Cold Stores in Hull which almost doubled total capacity.

The Group has continued to invest in new partnerships with Skipper Owners in Scotland and Peter & J. Johnstone Limited has also become a flourishing business.

J. Marr (Seafoods) Limited remains the Group's major subsidiary company and has developed into the UK's leading seafood trading business. The Company is very active throughout Russia, West and Eastern Europe, Africa, North America and the Far East.

Andrew Marr International has a strong management team and the Group is poised for further expansion and growth.

Chapter 12:
DIARY OF RECENT EVENTS

In September 1979 James Geoffrey Marr joined the Company and for a period of time worked at the Company's garage, the Flyover Service Station. Later an interest in agriculture prompted him to study farm management but in 1981 he returned to shipping, spending six months working for Seismographic Services Ltd., aboard the Marr vessel *Seisella*. With this insight into offshore operations he joined the Marr Vessel Management team and became involved in the day to day management of the world-wide fleet of survey vessels.

In April 1986, the decision was taken to broaden the Group's commercial interests in the leisure industry sector, a sector which was showing strong growth at the time. In July of that year James became the director responsible for the Company's overseas investment in Hotel Sotogrande SA: a Spanish hotel project and commercial property development.

Following the sale of the Spanish Company in 1992 to local interests James returned full time to the U.K. to resume an active role in the shipping and travel business leading to his present role as director of J. Marr Limited responsible for the two companies.

In 1993 James married Christine Gabler in her home town of Larcay, France.

On 31st December 1986 Her Majesty Queen Elizabeth II appointed Geoffrey Alan Marr a Commander of the Most Excellent Order of the British Empire.

Following the restructuring, on 16th February 1987, Mrs. Margaret Rose Elisabeth Marr and James Geoffrey Marr were appointed directors of the Company. Then, on 1st April 1987, the name of the Company was changed to J. Marr Ltd. In addition, three new groups were incorporated into the J. Marr Ltd. shareholding, namely: J. Marr (Shipping) Ltd., J. Marr (Fishing) Ltd., and J. Marr (Leisure) Ltd. Jim Hind was appointed a director of the shipping group, and in 1988 Nigel Atkins joined the board of the fishing group.

*Early on the morning of 3rd November 1994, prior to the sale of fish from the **Lancella** members of the Company meet to discuss market trends. Left to right: Skipper Malcolm Trott, Colin Robinson - fish salesman, Frank Knight - fish salesman, Charles Marr, Nigel Atkins.*

J. MARR & SON FLEET LIST (1870 —   )

NAME	P.L.N.	GROSS NET TONS	LENGTH BREADTH DEPTH	YEAR BUILT	BUILDER PLACE	NOTES
Sailing Smacks						
Adelaide	H	61.8	68.0 18.0 9.0	1870	Sandwich	Built new for Joseph Marr, 11.11.1870 at Sandwich. Sold for scrapping in 1889.
Earl of Mar	H825	72.3	73.0 19.0 10.0	1873	Brixham	Built for Joseph Marr, 11.8.1873 at Brixham. Sunk 25.1.1893, in collision in the North Sea.
Rachel Anne	H944	75.3	75.0 20.0 10.0	1875	Brixham	Built new for Joseph Marr, 28.7.1875 at Brixham. Sold 18.6.1894, to Norwegian owners.
Edith Louise	H1291	76.2	75.0 20.0 10.0	1880	Brixham	Built new for Joseph Marr, 18.9.1880 at Goole. Sold 14.8.1901, to Lawrence H. Ashton of Poole.
Emily Florence	H1312	78.9	76.0 20.0 10.0	1881	Brixham	Built new for Joseph Marr, 1.7.1881, at Brixham. Sold 25.2.1901, to John Forrest, of Peterhead.
Amy Isobel	H1367	86.1	79.0 21.0 11.0	1883	Brixham	Built new for Joseph Marr, 15.11.1883, at Brixham. Sold 3.3.1898, to Danish owners.
Lillian Maud	H1441	87.8	79.0 20.0 10.0	1885	Brixham	Built new for Joseph Marr, 13.4.1885, at Brixham. Sold 24.8.1901, to Spanish owners.
Mascotte	H1430	90.4	80.0 21.0 10.0	1885	Galmpton	Bought 5.4.1886 from Andrew Mudge, Hull. Sold 22.10.1889, to Norwegian owners.
Argument	H1185	76.9	75.0 20.0 10.0	1878	Goole	Bought 26.8.1889, from Thomas Moody, Hull. Sold 15.10.1889, to William S. Lowry, Hull. Sold 21.2.1903 to French owners.
Steam Trawlers						
Marrs	H172 FD31	154 64	100.8 20.5 11.0 11.0	1891	Beverley	First steam trawler built for Joseph Marr. Transferred to Fleetwood in 1898. Sold 1919, to French owners renamed *Le Barre*. Lost in collision in 1921.

NAME	P.L.N.	GROSS NET TONS	LENGTH BREADTH DEPTH	YEAR BUILT	BUILDER PLACE	NOTES
Lucerne	H399 FD34	154 60	106.0 20.6 10.9	1896	N. Shields	Sold 1915, to Aberdeen owners £7,750. Sunk by U-boat 19.5.1915 by time bombs. Position 50 miles NE by N from Rattray Head.
Annie	HL53 FD	152 56	105.8 20.9 10.9	1898	N. Shields	Sold 1905, to Spanish owners for £3,350. Renamed *Gero*. Scrapped in 1936.
Akranes	FD33	184 66	114.6 21.1 10.8	1899	N. Shields	Sold 1920, to Edward Baxter, Grimsby. Sold 1930, to Dutch owners renamed *Anna Josina*. Scrapped in 1936.
Rattler	H138 FD199	149 48	100.5 20.5 10.7	1891	Glasgow	Sold 1929, to J. W. Robinson, Fleetwood for £750. Scrapped in 1932.
Nile	GY500 FD11	174 45	111.0 21.1 11.0	1898	N. Shields	Bought December 1902, from Letten Bros. Grimsby for £3,400. Sold 1918, to T. J. Hancock, Milford Haven. Foundered October 1922.
Desideratum	H154 FD45	150 59	100.5 20.8 11.0	1891	Hull	Bought 1904, from London & Yorkshire Trawler & Fish Carrying Co., Hull. Sold 1914, to Swedish owners renamed *Pysen*. Scrapped in 1938.
Amy	FD39	223 79	125.0 22.0 12.1	1905	Goole	Mined off le Havre, 11.4.1917 whilst serving with the Royal Navy, on charter to the Admiralty.
Maud	FD40	223 79	125.0 22.0 12.1	1905	Goole	Sold 1907, to Rockliffe Steam Fishing Co., Fleetwood for £6,150. Wrecked February 1912, at Kynance, Lizard.
Evelyn	FD59	235 74	125.0 22.6 11.5	1906	Goole	Sold 1923, to H. A. Jeffries, Grimsby for £3,000. Stranded and sunk September 1936.
Mary	FD84	256 90	128.7 22.7 11.4	1906	Dundee	Sank 5.11.1914, after being mined off Yarmouth, whilst serving as a mine-sweeper with the Royal Navy. On charter to the Admiralty.
Margaret	FD92	297 117	135.0 23.0 12.0	1907	Goole	Sold June 1913, to the Admiralty. Resold 1914 to Dutch owners renamed *Tres Frates*. Deleted 1918 possible war loss.

NAME	P.L.N.	GROSS NET TONS	LENGTH BREADTH DEPTH	YEAR BUILT	BUILDER PLACE	NOTES
Elise x *Camperdown*	FD164	239 72	126.5 22.0 11.6	1907	Aberdeen	Bought 1914, from T. S. Kellsall. Sunk 22.8.1918, after being torpedoed off Blyth, whilst serving as a minesweeper with the Royal Navy. On charter to the Admiralty.
Ethel	FD173	278 99	130.0 22.6 12.1	1907	Goole	Bought 1913 from L. Cohen Fleetwood. For the Active Fishing Company. Sold 1920 to Icelandic owners as *Irvana*. Sold 1926 to Portuguese owners renamed *Apollo*. Scrapped in 1958 as *Cabo Juby*.
Diana	FD135	172 52	110.0 21.0 10.9	1899	Glasgow	Bought 1908, from W. Widdowson, Hull. For the Lancashire Fishing Company. Sold 1914 to the Nettle Fishing Co. Aberdeen for £2,250. Sold 1919, to R. S. Hewitt, London. Scrapped in 1936.
Neptune	FD124	172 52	110.0 21.0 10.9	1899	Glasgow	Bought 1908, from W. Widdowson, Hull. For the Lancashire Fishing Company. Sold 1920 to Norwegian owners renamed *Bordeyri*. Later *Torhav*. Scrapped in 1933.
Vera Grace	FD211	232 89	126.0 22.1 10.1	1908	Dundee	Sold 27.2.1941, to Thornton Trawlers Ltd., Fleetwood for £3,500. Scrapped in 1954.
Orontes	FD54	178 76	111.5 21.0 11.5	1895	Beverley	Bought 1908, from T. Hamling, Hull. For the Lancashire Fishing Company. Sold 1919 to Canadian owners. Sold 1920 to Grimsby owners. Scrapped 1937 in Holland.
Norbreck	FD30	201 57	121.3 21.6 11.7	1905	Aberdeen	Managed by J. Marr for the Norbreck Fishing Co. Sold 1920 to Direct Fish Supplies, Milford Haven. Served with the Royal Navy as a minesweeper in 1914-1918 and 1939-1945 Wars. Sank April 1946, as *Craigmiller* of Aberdeen.
Marton	FD38	232 80	125.3 21.7 11.8	1905	Aberdeen	Managed by J. Marr for the Norbreck Fishing Co. Sold 1920 to Direct Fish Supplies Milford Haven. Scrapped in 1923.
Thornton	FD41	225 71	125.5 21.9 8.8	1905	Aberdeen	Managed by J. Marr for the Norbreck Fishing Co. Sold 1920, to Bishop, Milford Haven. Scrapped in 1934.

NAME	P.L.N.	GROSS NET TONS	LENGTH BREADTH DEPTH	YEAR BUILT	BUILDER PLACE	NOTES
Tettenhall	FD43	227 72	125.7 21.9 8.8	1905	Aberdeen	Managed by J. Marr for the Tettenhall Fishing Co. Sank 23.5.1917, after being mined off Lowestoft, whilst serving with the Royal Navy as a minesweeper.
Newbridge	FD55	228 75	125.7 21.9 8.9	1906	Aberdeen	Managed by J. Marr for the Tettenhall Fishing Co. Sank 19.11.1917, following collision off Prawle Point, whilst serving as a minesweeper with the Royal Navy.
Boscobel	FD70	225 72	125.8 21.9 8.9	1906	Aberdeen	Managed by J. Marr for the Tettenhall Fishing Co. Sold 1920, to the Active Fishing Co. Sold 1929, to T. Walker Aberdeen. Foundered May 1937.
Merrydale	FD77	225 72	125.2 21.7 11.8	1906	Aberdeen	Managed by J. Marr for the Tettenhall Fishing Co. Sold 1923 to the Victory S. T. Co., Fleetwood. To Aberdeen 1929, scrapped 1937.
Wrenthorpe	FD80	225 74	125.4 21.7 9.0	1906	Aberdeen	Managed by J. Marr for the Tettenhall Fishing Co. Bought 1920, by J. Marr & Son. Sold 1929, to J. Baxter Aberdeen, for £2,500. Scrapped in 1937.
Kilda	FD144	243 93	126.7 23.0 9.7	1911	Goole	Sold 13.4.1914 to the Amiralty for £6,750. Renamed *Tubal Cain*. Sold 1923, to Bunch Fishing Co. Grimsby. Scrapped in 1938.
Phoebe	FD121	278 109	130.0 22.6 12.1	1907	Goole	Sold 1920, to Portuguese owners renamed *Cintra*. Sank off Lisbon November 1954 named *Exploratador Segundo*.
Romulus	H1483 FD128	159 76	109.0 20.2 10.6	1885	Beverley	Bought 24.11.1910 from Pickering & Haldanes, Hull. Sold 1918 to N. Blow, Grimsby. In 1920 converted to a dredger for use at Bristol. Scrapped in 1939.
Hercules	FD172	261 103	128.3 22.0 12.0	1903	Beverley	Bought 15.11.1912 from the Anglo-Norwegian Fishing Co. Hull. For the Lancashire Fishing Co. renamed *Hercules IV*. Sold in 1937, for £900. For scrapping at Preston.

Rattler FD199 1891-1929.

Vera Grace FD211 1908-1941.

Kilda FD144 1911-1914.

Hercules FD172 1913-1937.

NAME	P.L.N.	GROSS NET TONS	LENGTH BREADTH DEPTH	YEAR BUILT	BUILDER PLACE	NOTES
Socrates	FD185 H885	296 110	138.6 23.0 11.7	1906	Glasgow	Bought 15.11.1912 from E. Watt, Hull for £5,250, for the Lancashire Fishing Co. Wrecked 11.1.1913 at Castle Bay.
Wasp	H112 FD169	149 55	100.5 20.5 10.7	1890	Glasgow	Bought 15.11.1912 from the British Steam Trawling Co. Hull. Sold July 1914, to Swedish owners for £1,350. Renamed *Gunnar*. Sold 1927, to Danish owners. Scrapped in 1929.
Tarantula	H175	155 64	100.5 20.5 10.7	1891	Glasgow	Bought 15.11.1912 from the British Steam Trawling Co. Hull. Sold March 1913, to Dogger Bank Trawler Co. Scarborough for £1,575. Sunk 25.9.1916, by U-Boat 20 miles NE of Scarborough.
Moth	H139 FD167	149 55	100.5 20.5 10.7	1891	Glasgow	Bought 1.11.1912 by J. A. Robertson for the Lancashire Fishing Company from the British Steam Trawling Co. Hull. Sold 1915, to Swedish owners renamed *Gilbert*. Lost circa 1924.
Active	H191 FD157	149 62	102.4 20.6 11.0	1892	Beverley	Bought 10.5.1912 for the Active Fishing Co. from Pickering & Haldane Hull. Sunk by U-Boat April 1917 off St. Abbs Head.
Fly	H104 FD166	158 60	101.4 20.6 11.0	1890	Beverley	Bought 15.11.1912 for the Active Fishing Co. from the British Steam Trawling Co. Hull. Sold 1920, to Aberdeen owners. Scrapped in 1924.
Hornet	H113 FD168	149 48	100.5 20.5 10.7	1890	Glasgow	Bought 15.11.1912 for the Active Fishing Co. from the British Steam Trawling Co. Hull. Sold 1920, to Swedish owners renamed *Evald*. Sunk October 1925 following a collision.
Tasmania	H122	146 60	100.5 20.5 11.0	1891	Hull	Bought 18.11.1912 for the Active Fishing Co. from the Hull Fish and Ice Company. Sold 1918, to T. W. Robinson Aberdeen. Scrapped in 1924.

NAME	P.L.N.	GROSS NET TONS	LENGTH BREADTH DEPTH	YEAR BUILT	BUILDER PLACE	NOTES
Vera	H960	333 149	140.0 23.7 12.4	1907	Beverley	Bought 1923, from Fresh Fish Supplies, Hull. For the Lancashire Fishing Co. Wrecked 5.3.1925, at Myrdalssandur, South coast of Iceland.
Lucida (1)	FD103	243 93	126.7 23.0 9.7	1911	Goole	Sold 1913 to Portuguese owners. Renamed *Bicolho*. 1929, renamed *Almourer*. Scrapped in 1950.
Velia (1)	FD229	278 121	133.5 23.0 12.0	1912	Selby	Sold 1914 to Icelandic owners. Renamed *Njorbur*. Lost circa 1918.
Luneda (1)	FD230	288 116	130.0 23.0 12.7	1912	Selby	Built for the Lancashire Fishing Co. Requisitioned during 1914-1918 War for service with the Royal Navy. Returned to owners 1919. Wrecked 9.2.1937 on a reef off the coast of Islay. The *Luneda* ran aground during a snowstorm, her 12 crew were rescued by the coaster *Pibroch*.
Clotilde	FD232 GY352	289 114	130.2 23.5 12.6	1913	Selby	Built for the Active Fishing Co. at a cost of £7950. Requisitioned during 1914-1918 War for service with the Royal Navy. Also served as a minesweeper between 1940-1945, Pennant No. FY534. Sold 1945 to Wembley Fishing Co. Grimsby. Bought 1948, by the Dinas Fishing Co. Fleetwood. Sold 1952 to the Queen Steam Fishing Co. Grimsby. Scrapped in 1956.
Imelda	FD13	251 97	126.8 23.0 12.1	1914	Dundee	Requisitioned during the 1914-1918 War, returned to fishing 1919. Requisitioned December 1939, for use as a boom defence vessel Pennant No. Z.136. Returned in 1946 and sold 24.1.1947 to J. N. Connell, Coatbridge for scrap.
Lucida (2)	FD20	251 97	126.8 23.0 12.1	1914	Dundee	Requisitioned during the 1914-1918 War for service with the Royal Navy. Returned to owners 1919. Sold 1938, to George Robb, Aberdeen. Sunk 11.1.1940 after being mined.

Active FD157 1912-1917.

Clotilde FD232 1913-1945.

Plan of the **Clotilde.**

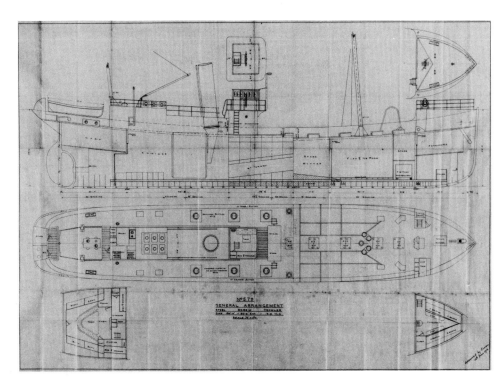

Alida *FD192 1915-1945.*

NAME	P.L.N.	GROSS NET TONS	LENGTH BREADTH DEPTH	YEAR BUILT	BUILDER PLACE	NOTES
Velia (2)	FD49	290 116	130.2 23.5 12.7	1914	Selby	Requisitioned during the 1914-1918 War for service with the Royal Navy. Returned to fishing 1919. Requisitioned in May 1940 as a minesweeper. Sunk 19.10.1940, after being mined off Harwich.
Alida	FD192	270 105	128.9 23.0 12.7	1915	Dundee	Built for the Lancashire Fishing Co. Went straight into service with the Royal Navy. Delivered to owners in 1919. Requisitioned again in 1940 for use as a boom defence vessel with the Royal Navy. Pennant No. Z.152. Returned in 1945 and subsequently scrapped in 1947.
Collena (1)	FD115	293 116	133.6 23.6 10.7	1915	Selby	Went straight into service with the Royal Navy. Delivered to owners in 1920. Requisitioned again in 1940 for use as a boom defence vessel with the Royal Navy Pennant No. Z.151. Returned to fishing in 1946. Was sold in 1942, to Aldred Fishing Co. Grimsby whilst under requisition. Sold 1950 to Swansea Trawlers renamed *Swansea Bay*. Scrapped in 1960 as *Rudilais* of Milford Haven.
Edwina (1)	FD205	267 104	127.2 23.0 12.7	1915	Dundee	Went straight into service with the Royal Navy. Delivered to owners 1919. Sold 1938 to the Dalby Fishing Co. Fleetwood. Served as a minesweeper with the Royal Navy 1940-1946 Pennant No. 4.134. Returned to owners 1946. Scrapped 1956.
Jacinta (1)	FD235	289 115	130.2 23.5 12.7	1915	Selby	Went straight into service with Royal Navy. Delivered to owners in 1919. Requisitioned again in 1940 for use as a minesweeper with the Royal Navy Pennant No. 4.138. Returned to fishing 1946. Was sold in 1944, to H. B. Ingram, Fleetwood for £10,500 whilst under requisition. Scrapped in 1953.

NAME	P.L.N.	GROSS NET TONS	LENGTH BREADTH DEPTH	YEAR BUILT	BUILDER PLACE	NOTES
Gavina (1)	FD236	289 115	130.2 23.5 12.8	1916	Selby	Went straight into service with Royal Navy Delivered to owners in 1919. Wrecked 5.10.1921 on Rathlin Island.
Anida	FD299	270 105	128.8 23.0 12.6	1917	Dundee	Went straight into service with Royal Navy. Delivered to owners in 1919. Wrecked 28.10.1924 in Islay Sound.
Dorinda (1)	FD198	270 105	128.8 23.0 12.6	1917	Dundee	Went straight into service with Royal Navy. Delivered to owners in 1919. Requisitioned again for the 1939-1945 War. Served as a minesweeper with the Royal Navy Pennant No. FY.623. Sold 1946, to the Anglo Steam Fishing Company Grimsby renamed *Anglo*. Scrapped 1956 as *Dernes*.
Idena (1)	FD288	270 105	128.8 23.0 12.6	1917	Dundee	Went straight into service with the Royal Navy. Abandoned and sunk by gunfire off Tromso 5.2.1918.
Norina (1) x *Pelican* x *Kunishi*	FD150	270 113	125.2 23.5 12.6	1917	Selby	Bought 1920, from French owners for £5,500. Renamed *Norina* 1929. Requisitioned for use as a boom defence vessel with the Royal Navy Pennant No. Z.145. Was sold 1942, to F. & T. Ross Hull, for £9,850, whilst under requisition. Scrapped in 1946.
Sir Mark Sykes	H43 FD410	307 124	136.7 23.2 12.3	1914	Selby	Bought 1922, from Pickering & Haldane's Hull, for £8,500. Sold 1928, to Argentinian owners for £8,000 renamed *Tito Bia*. Scrapped in 1957, named *Cie Pesca Aruaca*.
Shackleton	H1003 FD409	288 115	133.5 23.0 12.0	1913	Selby	Bought 1922, for the Lancashire Fishing Co Wrecked 1.3.1930 on Rathlin Island. All crew saved by local islanders.
Lord Minto	H105 FD51	295 123	136.7 23.2 12.3	1914	Selby	Bought 1925, for the Active Fishing Co. from The Yorkshire Fishing Co. Hull. Sunk 18.9.1939 by gunfire after being captured by a German submarine off the Flannan Islands. The crew having been transferred to the trawler *Nancy Hague* which was allowed to return to Fleetwood.

Sir Mark Sykes FD410/H43 1922-1928.

Irvana FD181 1928-1942.

Cordela FD120 1930-1946.

Corena FD195 1933-1946.

NAME	P.L.N.	GROSS NET TONS	LENGTH BREADTH DEPTH	YEAR BUILT	BUILDER PLACE	NOTES
Rosa Maris (1)	FD43	237 92	117.4 22.0 12.7	1920	Beverley	Bought 1926, for the Lancashire Fishing Co from the Wilberforce Fishing Co. Hull. Wrecked 16.1.1929 on Red Rocks, Eriskey Sound.
Hildina (1) x Hiddenite x Cavendish x William Leek	FD180 H226	276 123	125.5 23.5 12.7	1918	S. Shields	Bought 30.6.1928 from Kingston Steam Trawling Co. Hull for £5,750. Renamed Hildina in 1929. Requisitioned for service with the Royal Navy as a minesweeper between 1939-1946, Pennant No. FY.541. Returned to owners in 1946. Sold 1947, to Brixham Trawlers Fleetwood for £19,850, renamed Aigret. Scrapped in 1956.
Irvana (1) x Avanturine x Arthur Lessimore	FD181 H15	276 107	125.5 23.4 12.8	1917	Middlesbro'	Bought 30.6.1928 from Kingston Steam Trawling Co. Hull, for £5,750. Renamed Irvana in 1929. Requisitioned in 1940 for use as a minesweeper with the Royal Navy, Pennant No. FY.663. Sunk 16.1.1942, by German aircraft off Great Yarmouth.
Marsona x James Christopher	FD21	276 109	125.3 23.4 12.6	1918	S. Shields	Bought 28.2.1929 from Brand & Curzon Ltd. renamed Marsona. Requisitioned in 1939 for use as a minesweeper with the Royal Navy, Pennant No. FY.714. Sank 4.8.1940 after being mined off Cromarty.
Teroma x Isaac Heath	FD17	276 109	125.2 23.4 12.6	1918	S. Shields	Bought 28.2.1929 from Brand & Curzon Ltd., renamed Teroma. Requisitioned for service with the Royal Navy as a minesweeper between 1939-1945 Pennant No. FY.527. Returned to owners in 1945. Sold 1953, to Mason Trawlers, Fleetwood. Scrapped in 1958.
Criscilla (1)	FD23	350 136	135.4 25.0 13.4	1929	Selby	Stranded 3.11.1931 on Black Rock, Sound of Islay. Became a total loss.

NAME	P.L.N.	GROSS NET TONS	LENGTH BREADTH DEPTH	YEAR BUILT	BUILDER PLACE	NOTES
Maretta (1)	FD45	350 136	135.4 25.0 13.4	1929	Selby	Requisitioned for service with the Royal Navy as a minesweeper between 1939-1945 Pennant No. FY.665. Returned to fishing 1946. Was sold 1944, to the Iago Steam Trawlers, Fleetwood, for £18,500 whilst under requisition. Sold 1946 to United Trawlers Fleetwood. Sold 1953 to Dinas Fishing Company. Scrapped in 1959.
Armana (1)	FD121 H302	375 145	151.5 25.0 13.4	1930	Selby	This class of trawler cost £15,090 to build. Requisitioned for service with the Royal Navy as an auxiliary patrol vessel between 1940-1945 Pennant No. FY.1809. Returned 1945. Sold 18.2.1946, to Hull Merchants Amalgamated Trawlers, for £35,000 renamed *Bardia*. Scrapped in 1954.
Clevela	FD94 H160	355 140	140.4 25.0 13.4	1930	Selby	Requisitioned for service with the Royal Navy as a minesweeper between 1939-1946 Pennant No. FY.678. Returned to fishing 1947. Sold 1948, to Iago Steam Fishing Co. Fleetwood renamed *Red Plume*. Scrapped 1955.
Cordela	FD120 H242	355 139	140.4 25.0 13.4	1930	Selby	Requisitioned for service with the Royal Navy as a minesweeper between 1939-1946 Pennant No. FY.713. Sold 1946, to Hellyer Bros. Hull, renamed *Hausa*. Scrapped in 1954.
Fyldea (1)	FD72 H201	377 149	151.5 25.0 13.4	1930	Selby	Requisitioned for service with the Royal Navy as a minesweeper between 1939-1945 Pennant No. FY.666. Returned to Marr's in 1946. Sold 25.8.1946 to Ocean Steam Trawling Co. Hull, renamed *Howard*. Sold 1948, to Iago Fishing Company, Fleetwood renamed *Red Dragon*. Scrapped in 1958.

NAME	P.L.N.	GROSS NET TONS	LENGTH BREADTH DEPTH	YEAR BUILT	BUILDER PLACE	NOTES
Arlita x Castlethorpe x Lord Mersey	FD188 H427	326 134	138.5 23.7 12.8	1916	Selby	Bought 1.6.1933 from Alan Spilman, London for £4,100. Renamed Arlita. Sunk 18.9.1939 by gunfire, after being captured by a German submarine off the Flannan Islands, the crew having been transferred to the Fleetwood trawler Nancy Hague which was allowed to return to Fleetwood.
Corena (1) x Andalusite	FD195 H90	352 144	140.3 24.0 12.9	1924	Beverley	Bought 3.10.1933 from Kingston Steam Trawling Co. Hull for £7,600. Renamed Corena. Requisitioned for service with the Royal Navy as a minesweeper between 1939-1946. Pennant No. FY.709. Returned to fishing in 1946 and sold to J. Craig, Aberdeen. Scrapped in 1949.
Orilla x Andradite	FD191 H176	352 150	140.3 24.0 12.9	1925	Beverley	Bought 3.10.1933 from Kingston Steam Trawling Co. Hull for £7,400. Renamed Orilla. Sold 1939, to Faroese owners for £5,000 renamed Vesturvardi. Sold 1952, to Polish owners renamed Maly Woz. Scrapped in 1964.
Lord Gainford x Christopher Dixon	FD74 H73	324 131	138.5 23.7 12.8	1918	Selby	Bought 1.3.1934 from Robson Trawlers Ltd. Fleetwood for £3,900. Requisitioned for service with the Royal Navy as a boom defence vessel between 1939-1946 Pennant No. Z.111. Sold 1947, to J. P. Holman, Sierra Leone. Scrapped in 1955.
Botanic	H463	348 138	140.3 24.0 13.3	1928	Selby	Bought 3.5.1934 from the City Steam Fishing Co. Hull for £8,000. Requisitioned in 1939 for service with the Royal Navy as a minesweeper Pennant No. FY.707. Sunk 18.2.1942 bombed by enemy aircraft in the North Sea.
Dairycoates	H270	350 141	140.3 24.0 13.3	1926	Selby	Bought 3.5.1934 from the City Steam Fishing Co. Hull for £7,350. Bought by the Admiralty in 1939 for use as a boom defence vessel Pennant No. Z.44. Sold 1946 by the Admiralty to J. Craig Aberdeen. Sold 1948 to Dutch owners renamed Klaas Wykea. Scrapped in 1958.

NAME	P.L.N.	GROSS NET TONS	LENGTH BREADTH DEPTH	YEAR BUILT	BUILDER PLACE	NOTES
Westella (1)	H124	413 160	152.8 25.6 13.0	1934	Selby	First new trawler built for the City Steam Fishing by J. Marr & Son Ltd. Sold 31.8.1939 to the Admiralty for conversion to an anti submarine patrol vessel. Pennant No. FY.161. Sunk 2.6.1940 after being mined in the English Channel.
Northcoates x *Zircon* x *George Corton*	H329	277 107	125.4 23.5 12.6	1919	Falmouth	Bought 27.5.1935 from Kingston Steam Trawling Co. Hull for £3,800, for the City Steam Fishing Co. renamed *Northcoates*. Requisitioned in 1939 for service with the Royal Navy as a minesweeper Pennant No. FY.548 Sank in tow 2.12.1944 after springing a leak in bad weather in the English Channel.
Eastcoates x *Ruby* x *John Graham*	H393	277 108	125.5 23.5 12.7	1919	Beverley	Bought 27.5.1935 from Kingston Steam Trawling Co. Hull for £4,000 for the City Steam Fishing Co. Hull, renamed *Eastcoates*. Requisitioned for service with the Royal Navy as a minesweeper between 1939-1945 Pennant No. FY.1771. Returned to owners 1945. Sold 28.4.1947 to Odafoam Ltd., for £71,500. Bought back 3.8.1950 by J. Marr and Son Ltd., for £2,750. Scrapped in 1955.
Southcoates x *Rhodolite* x *Samuel Drake*	H5	276 108	125.7 23.4 12.8	1918	Paisley	Bought 27.5.1935 from Kingston Steam Trawling Co. Hull for £3,800 for the City Steam Fishing Co. Hull, renamed *Southcoates*. Requisitioned for service with the Royal Navy as an auxiliary patrol vessel between 1940-1945 Pennant No. 4.140. Returned in 1945. Sold 24.1.1946 to J. R. Heperworth, Paull near Hull for scrapping.
Westcoates x *Lord Ancaster* x *James Wright*	H662	326 130	138.5 23.7 12.8	1918	Selby	Bought 15.7.1935 from Pickering & Haldanes Hull for £4,500 for the City Steam Fishing Co. Hull. Sold 1939 to Loch Fishing Co. Hull for £3,000 renamed *Loch Moidart*. Requisitioned for service with the Royal Navy as an auxiliary patrol vessel between 1940-1946 Pennant No. 4.229. Sold 1947 for scrapping.

Continued on page 97

Lord Gainford FD74 1934-1947.

Southcoates H5 1935-1946.

*The whaler **William Lee** in the Arctic circa 1831-32, by the artist John Ward
from the collection of the Hull Town Docks Museum.*

The *Westella* H124 1934-1940 by Adrian Thompson.

The *Lancella* H290 1953-1977.

Maretta FD245 1965-1977.

Swanella H421 1967-1981
Photographed in Falmouth Bay during the
Mackerel fishing season May 1980.

Norina FD324. Built 1975 still part of the Company's fishing fleet.

Thornella H96. Built 1988 still part of the Company's fishing fleet.

Swanella H142 1988-1993
a pelagic freezer vessel.

Southella H240.
Part of the Company's present fleet.

*The **Swanella** H1065 under the temporary name of **Irvana** in 1994.*

*Vessels of the Cordella group at Grytviken Hardor, South Georgia on 27th May 1982, transferring the 7th Gurkha Rifles and the 16th Field Ambulance and their equipment from the liner **Queen Elizabeth II** to the liner **Canberra** and the ferry **Norland** prior to the latter vessels return to San Carlos water on 1st June 1982 during the Falklands War.*

*The former trawler **Marbella** now **Northern Horizon** seen in her present form after a recent conversion.*

*The former trawler **Benella** H132 in her role as a Safety Standby vessel.*

*The former trawler **Southella** H40 on her way to the Falklands under the name of **Falklands Desire**.*

*The **Northella** in her M. o. D. livery.*

*The former trawler **Farnella** H135
in her survey role.*

*The **Cordella** recently bought back from New Zealand owners.*

*The fishery research vessel **Eastella**.*

Falklands Right *former West German fishery research vessel.*

*The fishery patrol vessel **Criscilla**.*

*The survey research vessel **HV. Fox**.*

NAME	P.L.N.	GROSS NET TONS	LENGTH BREADTH DEPTH	YEAR BUILT	BUILDER PLACE	NOTES
Kirkella (1)	H319 H155 GY592 FD7	435 170	157.8 26.1 14.1	1936	Selby	Cost £15,950 to build. Sold 31.8.1939, to the Admiralty for conversion to an anti submarine patrol vessel Pennant No. FY.174. Bought back from the Admiralty in 1946. Sold 17.12.1947 to the Dinas steam Trawling Co. Fleetwood, for £67,500. Sold 1952, to Sir Basil Parkes (Grimsby) renamed *St. Benedict*. Sold 1957 to the Cevic Fishing Co. Fleetwood, renamed *Reneva*. Scrapped in 1960.
Joseph Button	M272	290 119	125.5 23.7 12.7	1918	Beverley	Bought 31.7.1939 from Milford Fisheries Ltd. Milford Haven for £3,750. Requisitioned 8.1939 for service with the Royal Navy as a minesweeper. Sunk 22.10.1940 after being mined off Aldeburgh, Suffolk.
Robert Bowen	M269	290 127	125.5 23.6 12.7	1918	Beverley	Bought 31.7.1939 from Milford Fisheries Ltd. Milford Haven for £3,650. Requisitioned 8.1939 for service with the Royal Navy as a minesweeper. Sunk 9.10.1940 by enemy aircraft off Aberdeen. (One of three vessels sunk in the same attack).
E & F x *James Green*	M252	275 107	125.5 23.4 12.8	1917	Middlesbro'	Bought 30.9.1939 from Miss Elizabeth Owens, Milford Haven for £5,750. Requisitioned 1940 by the Admiralty for use as a boom defence vessel renamed H.M.T. *Laverock* Pennant No. Z.240. Delivered to Marr's in 1946, sold 24.1.1947 to Marine Metals, London for scrapping.
Thomas Deas x *James Johnson*	M253	276 107	125.5 23.4 12.8	1917	Middlesbro'	Bought 30.9.1939 from Miss Elizabeth Owens, Milford Haven for £5,750. Sunk 16.2.1941 after being mined 4 miles off Spurn Point.
Drusilla	A133	250 96	125.0 23.5 12.4	1914	Middlesbro'	Bought 31.10.1939 by the City Fishing Co. from the North Star Fishing Co. Aberdeen for £4,750. Sold 18.1.1945 to Eton Fishing Co. Hull, for £18,500. Sold 1948 to Alfred Bannister, Grimsby. Scrapped in 1959.

NAME	P.L.N.	GROSS NET TONS	LENGTH BREADTH DEPTH	YEAR BUILT	BUILDER PLACE	NOTES
Regnault	H156 GY46	208 82	115.3 22.2 13.4	1913	S. Shields	Bought 4.1940 by the Active Fishing Co. from Richard Irvin, N. Shields. Sold 1943 to J. Bennet, Hull. Sold 1945 to the Anglo Steam Fishing Co. Grimsby. 1951 renamed *Inganes*. Scrapped in 1953.
Celtia	LL28	239 93	120.3 21.6 11.6	1907	N. Shields	Bought 18.1.1941 by the City Fishing Co. from Yolland and Llewellyn, Milford Haven for £6.425. Sold 5.8.1944 to Wyre Steam Trawling Co. Fleetwood for £12,500. Scrapped in Dublin in 1955.
Triton	GY384	230 87	120.0 21.9 11.4	1907	Dundee	Bought 31.1.1941 from Charles Dobson, Grimsby for £6,000, whilst under requisition. Served as an auxiliary patrol vessel with the Royal Navy between 1939-1945 Pennant No. Y.742. Returned in 1946 and sold to John Lee, Belfast for scrap.
Dewsland	FD64	236 93	120.0 21.7 11.6	1907	Selby	Bought 31.1.1941 from Alexander Keay, Fleetwood for £6,500. Free to fish during War. Sold 1944, to Hull Merchants Amalgamated Trawlers for £12,000 renamed *Derna*. Sold 1953 to South African owners. Wrecked 14.9.1954 at Mombassa.
Bahama x *Tom Melling*	FD414	270 93	125.7 22.1 12.0	1907	Middlesbro'	Bought 31.1.1941 from Alexander Keay, Fleetwood for £7,500. Free to fish during War. Sold 4.5.1942 to Crampin Fishing Co. Grimsby for £8,600. Scrapped in 1956.
Ugiebank	GY393	204 79	117.3 22.0 12.2	1913	Aberdeen	Bought 15.3.1941 by the Active Fishing Co. from the Peterhead Trawling Co. whilst under requisition. Served as an auxiliary patrol vessel between 1939-1945 Pennant No. 4.430. Sold 1943 to J. Bennet, Peterhead. Sold 1948 to A. G. Hamer, Grimsby. Scrapped in 1951.

Dewsland FD64 1941-1944.

Ben Bheula A422 1942-1946.

NAME	P.L.N.	GROSS NET TONS	LENGTH BREADTH DEPTH	YEAR BUILT	BUILDER PLACE	NOTES
Tamora x William Loft	H853	275 113	125.3 23.4 12.6	1920	S. Shields	Bought 3.9.1941 by the City Fishing Co. from Hendersons Trawling Co. Hull for £8,200. whilst under requisition. Served as a minesweeper with the Royal Navy between 1939-1945 Pennant No. FY.643. Delivered in 1946. Sold 10.6.1947 to Dublin Trawling & Cold Store Co. for £18,500. Scrapped in 1954.
Dagon x Hatsuse	GY438	282 110	128.5 23.5 12.6	1920	Beverley	Bought 31.10.1941 from Consolidated Fisheries Ltd. Grimsby for £14,500. Sold 25.9.45 to A. J. Tilbrook Ltd. Milford Haven for £18,500. Sold 1952 to Aberdeen owners renamed Casimir. Scrapped in 1955.
Zonia x Apollo	LT118	150 58	100.6 20.5 10.7	1898	Glasgow	Bought 31.10.1941 from Consolidated Fisheries Ltd. Grimsby for £3,850. Sold 3.8.1945, to Samuel Stuart, London. Scrapped in 1951.
Croton	LT84	150 58	100.6 20.5 10.7	1898	Glasgow	Bought 31.10.1941 from Consolidated Fisheries Ltd. Grimsby for £3,850. Sold 21.7.45 to Partnership (Hull) Ltd. for £4,000. Scrapped in 1950.
Wargrey	GY516	246 97	117.4 22.0 12.7	1917	Beverley	Bought 31.10.1941 by the City Fishing Co. from Arctic Steam Fishing Co. Grimsby for £10,500. Sold 8.7.1942 to Hudson Brothers Trawlers Hull for £13,000. Sold 1946 to Hull Merchants Amalgamated Trawlers renamed Tobruk. Sold 1950 to Aberdeen owners renamed G. D. Taylor. Scrapped in 1955.
Kingsway	GY37	211 83	115.4 21.6 11.5	1905	Beverley	Bought 24.12.1941 by the City Fishing Co. from Charles Dobson, Grimsby for £6,400. Sold 22.9.1943 to Scarborough owners for £9,750. Scrapped in 1953.
Donalda	GY149 GY78	226 113	117.0 22.0 12.7	1914	Beverley	Bought 1.1.1942 by the Active Fishing Co. from Sir Alec Black, Bart. Grimsby. Sold 1.8.1942 to Hudson Steam Fishing Co. Hull. Sold 1945 to Grimsby Motor Trawlers. Scrapped in 1957.

NAME	P.L.N.	GROSS NET TONS	LENGTH BREADTH DEPTH	YEAR BUILT	BUILDER PLACE	NOTES
Fairway x *Lord Knaresborough* x *Richard Jewell*	FD140 H130 GY488	312 130	138.5 23.7 12.8	1918	Selby	Bought 22.1.1942 from Rinovia Fishing Co. Grimsby for £9,250. Under Govt. requisition. Served with the Royal Navy as a minesweeper between 1940-1946 Pennant No. 4.33. Returned to Marr's in 1946. Scrapped in 1955.
Andanes x *Wimpole*	GY923	320 163	137.0 23.5 12.9	1916	Selby	Bought 22.1.1942 from Drangey Fishing Co Grimsby for £8,000. Under Govt. requisition. Served with the Royal Navy as a boom defence vessel between 1940-1946 Pennant No. 4.151. Delivered to Marr's in 1946. Sold 24.1.1947 to Marine Metals London for scrapping.
Ben Bheula x *Leonato* x *Thomas Dowding*	A422	275 108	125.6 23.4 12.6	1917	S. Shields	Bought 13.1.1942 from Richard Irvin & Sons Ltd. North Shields for £8,200. Served with the Royal Navy as a minesweeper between 1939-1945 Pennant No. FY.1681. Returned to Marr's 1946 and sold to Pegasus Trawling Co. Fleetwood for £20,000. Scrapped in 1953.
William Bell	LO201	290 119	125.5 23.5 12.7	1918	Beverley	Bought 15.1.1942 from the Mills Steamship Co. London for £8,625. Under Govt. requisition, Served with the Royal Navy as a minesweeper between 1940-1946 Pennant No. FY.1727. Returned to Marr's in 1946 and sold to W. H. Arnott, Glasgow for scrapping.
James Lay	LO333	278 121	125.0 23.5 12.7	1918	London	Bought 15.1.1942 from the Mills Steamship Co. London for £8,625. Under Government requisition. Served with the Royal Navy as a minesweeper between 1939-1944. This trawler was the first to be delivered back to Marr's from war time service. Sold 11.3.1946 to Dinas Steam Trawling Co. for £19,000. Scrapped in 1960.

NAME	P.L.N.	GROSS NET TONS	LENGTH BREADTH DEPTH	YEAR BUILT	BUILDER PLACE	NOTES
Thomas Altoft	H132	290 127	125.5 23.5 12.7	1919	Beverley	Bought 15.1.1942 from the Mills Steamship Co. London for £8,625. Under Government requisition. Served with the Royal Navy as a minesweeper between 1939-1946 Pennant No. FY.552. Delivered to Marr's in 1946. Wrecked 8.11.1947 on Glas Island, Scalpey, Harris. All the crew were saved.
Ben Dearg x *Turcoman* x *Daily Express* x *Thomas Alexander*	FD286 A416	280 109	125.5 23.5 12.7	1920	Beverley	Bought 6.3.1942 from Richard Irvin & Sons Ltd. North Shields for £8,900. Under Government requisition. Served with the Royal Navy as a minesweeper between 1939-1946 Pennant No. FY.690. Delivered to Marr's in 1946. Sold 1.7.1949 to the Anglo-Australian Fishing Co. for £15,000. Sunk 1953 used as a target by the Royal Australian Navy.
Saronta x *Vambery*	H390 GY1082	316 127	135.3 23.5 12.3	1917	Selby	Bought 22.4.1942 from Sir Alec Black, Bart. Grimsby for £8,500. Under Government requisition. Served with the Royal Navy as a minesweeper between 1940-1945 Pennant No. FY.1849. Sold 1945 to Shire Trawlers Grimsby for £14,000. Sold 1947 to Lord Line Hull. Scrapped in 1952.
Wyoming x *Veresis*	GY483	302 157	135.0 23.5 12.3	1915	Selby	Bought 22.4.1942 from Sir Alec Black, Bart. Grimsby for £8,100. Under Government requisition. Requisitioned for service with the Royal Navy as a minesweeper in 1939 Pennant No. FY.1862. Sank 20.5.1944 after being mined off Harwich.
Lady Eleanor x *Clee Ness* x *Thomas Jago*	H691	324 128	138.5 23.7 12.8	1918	Selby	Bought 13.9.1942 from Jutland Amalgamated Trawlers Hull for £12,500. Under Govt. requisition. Served with the Royal Navy as a boom defence vessel between 1940-1946 Pennant No. Z.157. Returned to Marr's in 1946. Sold 24.1.1947 to J. N. Connell, Coatbridge for scrapping.

NAME	P.L.N.	GROSS NET TONS	LENGTH BREADTH DEPTH	YEAR BUILT	BUILDER PLACE	NOTES
Rilette	LH35	212 82	115.5 22.1 11.9	1917	Aberdeen	Bought 31.9.1942 from Thomas H. Scales, Leith for £10,250. Free to fish during War. Sold 1945, to G. C. Wilson Grimsby for £13,000. Sold to Aberdeen owners 1949. Scrapped 1960.
Craig Island x *Marthe*	LH141	243 91	120.2 22.0 12.0	1913	Beverley	Bought 31.9.1942 from Thomas H. Scales, Leith for £7,250. Under Govt. requisition. Served with the Royal Navy as a boom defence vessel between 1939-1944 Pennant No. Z.157. Sold 1946 to J. Cameron Peterhead for scrap.
Eileen Wayman x *Southern Prince*	H235	194 86	115.6 22.0 11.8	1914	Willington-on-Tyne	Bought in 22.2.1944 by the Active Fishing Co. from Fillets Ltd. Hull. Wrecked 8.12.45 at Grannan Point, Isle of Lewis.
Darnett Ness x *Jade* x *Thomas Boudige*	H340	277 109	125.5 23.5 12.8	1920	Beverley	Bought 25.10.1944 from the Trident Steam Fishing Co. Hull for £11,750. Under Govt. requisition. Served with the Royal Navy as a minesweeper between 1939-1945 Pennant No. FY.542. Returned to Marr's in 1946, sold 1956 to Hammond Lane Metal Co. Dublin for scrapping.
North Ness x *Alexandrite* x *Alexander Sack*	H11	275 107	125.5 23.4 12.8	1917	Middlesbro'	Bought 25.10.1944 from the Trident Steam Fishing Co. Hull for £10,550. Under Govt. requisition. Served with the Royal Navy as an auxiliary patrol vessel between 1940-1946 Pennant No. 4.100. Returned to Marr's in 1946. Sold 22.6.1949 to H. B. Ingram Milford Haven for £13,000. Scrapped in 1956.
Marinda	FD155	342 124	136.0 24.6 13.9	1946	Aberdeen	First new post war trawler built for J. Marr and Son Ltd. delivered 14.1.46. Sold 3.2.47 to the Seddon Fishing Co. for £54,000. Bought 2.8.1949 back from the Seddon Fishing Co. for £35,000. Sold 26.10.1950 to the National Trawling & Fishing Co. Cape Town for £40,000. Sunk 1968 used as a target by the South African Navy.

James Lay LO333 1942-1946.

Marinda FD155 1947-1950.

*Plan of the **Northella (1)** H244 1946-1948.*

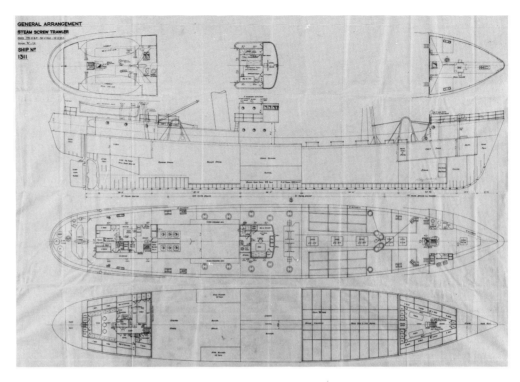

Southella H303 1946-1965.

NAME	P.L.N.	GROSS NET TONS	LENGTH BREADTH DEPTH	YEAR BUILT	BUILDER PLACE	NOTES
Josena (1)	H207	361 139	136.1 25.2 13.2	1946	Beverley	Sold 1947 to the Polish Government for their fishing fleet. Renamed *Syriusz*. Scrapped in 1969.
Iolite x *Navena (1)*	FD149 H372	361 139	136.1 25.2 13.2	1946	Beverley	Sold 24.12.1946 to Kingston Steam Trawling Co. Hull for £55,000 renamed *Iolite*. Bought back on 11.8.1949 for £72,000. Sold 9.2.1951 to the National Trawling & Fishing Co. of Cape Town for £42,000. Scuttled in 1969 at False Bay, Cape Town to form an artificial reef to attract shoals of fish.
Borella	H240	524 186	179.5 27.7 14.4	1946	Beverley	First post war deep water trawler built for J. Marr and Son Ltd. at a cost of £72,500. Sold 1953, to National Fishing Co. Cape Town South Africa, for £70,000. Scuttled in 1971.
Northella (1)	H244	579 216	177.9 30.2 15.1	1946	Selby	Built at a cost of £65,125. Sold 25.6.1948 to East Riding Trawlers a subsidiary of Charleson-Smith for £117,500 renamed *Stella Canopus*. Sailed from Hull 22.7.1967 for scrapping at Ghent.
Southella (1)	H303	536 191	181.2 27.2 14.4	1946	Beverley	The first oil burner built for J. Marr and Son Ltd., at a cost of £66,851. This fine trawler was retained by the Company all its working life, this was a rarity as most older trawlers were sold out of the fleet. Sold 18.1.1965 to Van Heyghen Freris, Ghent for scrapping for £6,400.
Carella x H.M.T. *Ruby* x *Cape Bathurst*	H4 FD319	421 162	152.1 25.6 13.6	1933	Selby	This trawler was the first to be built with a cruiser stern. She was bought by the Admiralty in 1935 and converted into a Gem Class anti submarine vessel. Bought 26.4.1946 from the Admiralty for £12,650. Refitted for fishing and renamed *Carella*. Sold 3.12.1948 to Hendersons Trawlers for £61,000. Sold 1953 to Dinas Steam Trawling Co. Scrapped in 1959.

NAME	P.L.N.	GROSS NET TONS	LENGTH BREADTH DEPTH	YEAR BUILT	BUILDER PLACE	NOTES
Westella (2) x H.M.T. *Pearl* x *Dervish*	H349 FD318	426 160	154.6 25.6 13.9	1934	Beverley	This trawler was bought in 1935 by the Admiralty and converted into a Gem Class anti submarine vessel. Bought 9.4.1946 from the Admiralty for £14,500. Refitted for fishing and renamed *Westella*. (Replacing the trawler lost in the War). Sold 25.6.1948 to the Pegasus Fishing Co. for £67,000. Sold 1953, to the Dinas Steam Trawling Co. Scrapped in 1959.
mv. *Thorina*	H318	315 114	136.8 25.6 12.6	1946	Beverley	Sold 1947 to N.V. Vissch, Ymuiden Holland Bought 1962 by Claridge Trawlers Lowestoft renamed *St. Georges*. Scrapped in 1981 after being scuttled during the making of the James Bond film "For Your Eyes Only".
Lorella	H455	558 201	170.8 29.2 14.2	1947	Beverley	Lost 26.1.1955 off the North Cape of Iceland in severe weather along with the *Roderigo*. All 40 crewmen were lost from the two ships, a tragedy which stunned the whole of Britain.
Murella	H481	550 200	171.0 29.2 14.7	1947	Selby	Cost £81,920 to build for the Trident Steam Fishing Co. Sold 1951 to Loch Steam Fishing Co. Hull renamed *Loch Moidart*. Transferred to Fleetwood in 1967. Scrapped in 1968.
Junella (1)	H497	550 200	171.0 29.2 14.7	1948	Selby	Sold 11.4.1949 to Alsey Steam Fishing Co. Grimsby for £129,500 renamed *Kirknes*. Taken over by Ross Group 1960 renamed *Ross Hunter*. Scrapped in 1964.
Cordella (1)	H572	604 222	170.4 29.2 14.3	1948	Aberdeen	Cost £84,304 to build. Retained by the Company all her working life. Sold 3.8.1965 Jes de Smedt Antwerp for scrap at a price of £8,050.
Thornella (1)	H582	604 222	170.4 29.2 14.3	1948	Aberdeen	Cost £84,220 to build. Sold 1954 to Hellyer Bros. Hull renamed *Banquo*. Transferred briefly to Fleetwood in 1967. Scrapped 9.1967 at Ghent.

Lorella H455 1947-1955.

Cordella (1) *H572 1948-1965.*

Daniel Clowden FD280 1948-1952.

Swanella H42 1949-1952.

NAME	P.L.N.	GROSS NET TONS	LENGTH BREADTH DEPTH	YEAR BUILT	BUILDER PLACE	NOTES
Commiles x *Daily Herald* x *Admiral Marquer* x *Matthew Flynn*	FD285	276 108	125.6 23.4 12.6	1918	S. Shields	Bought 28.11.1947 from Shire Trawlers Ltd for £12,500. Sold 8.6.1949 to the Anglo-Australian Trawlers (Pty) Ltd., for £15,000. Sunk 1953 used as a target by the Royal Australian Navy.
Concentrator x *River Kent* x *John Thorling*	FD276	276 107	125.5 23.4 12.8	1917	Middlesbro'	Bought 8.7.1948 from Yolland Bros. Ltd., Milford Haven for £12,500. Sold 9.3.1951 to Stephen Fishing Co. Aberdeen. Scrapped in 1959.
Tenedos x *Dominick Addison*	FD277	290 126	125.5 23.5 12.7	1919	Beverley	Bought 8.7.1948 from Yolland Bros. Ltd., Milford Haven for £13,132. Sold 1952 to the Japan Fishing Co. Grimsby for £7,500 renamed *Hondo*. Scrapped in 1960.
George Adgell	FD368	290 126	125.5 23.5 13.7	1919	Beverley	Bought 8.7.1948 from Yolland Bros. Ltd., Milford Haven for £13,086. Sold 14.7.1953 to the British Iron & Steel Corporation for scrapping.
William Mannel	LO370	276 107	125.5 23.4 12.8	1917	Middlesbro'	Bought 13.9.1948 from Yolland Bros. Ltd., Milford Haven for £12,500. Stranded 22.2.1949 off Portaleen, Donegal, refloated on the afternoon tide but sank whilst in tow of the trawler *Gava*. All the crew were saved.
Daniel Clowden	FD280	280 113	125.6 23.5 14.1	1919	Greenock	Bought 13.8.1948 from Haven Trawlers Ltd. for £13,698. Sold 13.12.1952 to the British Iron & Steel Corporation for scrapping.
George Cousins	FD287	276 122	125.0 23.5 12.8	1919	Ayr	Bought 13.8.1948 from Haven Trawlers Ltd. for £12,500. Sold 5.4.1951 to Harrow Baxter Steam Fishing Co. Aberdeen for £7,700. Scrapped in 1956.
Cotsmuir x *Thomas Gable*	FD284	275 107	125.5 23.4 12.8	1917	Middlesbro'	Bought 29.9.1948 from J.C. Llewellyn Ltd., Milford Haven for £13,890. Sold 2.2.1952 to David Wood Aberdeen for £7,700. Scrapped in 1959.
T. R. Ferens	FD282	279 108	125.7 23.4 12.8	1918	Paisley	Bought 29.9.1948 from J.C. Lewellyn Ltd., Milford Haven for £13,861. Scrapped in 1953.

NAME	P.L.N.	GROSS NET TONS	LENGTH BREADTH DEPTH	YEAR BUILT	BUILDER PLACE	NOTES
Benella (1)	H15	666 235	180.5 30.1 15.1	1949	Aberdeen	Built for the Trident Steam Fishing Co. Sold 1951 to Newington Steam Trawling Co. renamed *James Barrie*. Wrecked 27.3.1969 on Louther Skerry, Pentland Firth whilst outward bound for Iceland. Her crew were rescued by the Wick lifeboat.
Farnella (1)	H41	684 246	181.7 30.6 15.1	1949	Beverley	Cost £102,522 to build. Sold 12.1.1952 to Kingston Steam Trawling Co. Hull for £145,000, renamed *Kingston Andalusite*. Scrapped in 1969.
Primella (1)	H103	665 234	180.5 30.1 15.1	1949	Aberdeen	Cost £114,445 to build. Sold 31.5.1957 to Newington Steam Trawling Co. Hull, for £125,000 renamed *Peter Scott*. Scrapped in 1974 at Spain.
Starella (1)	H75	683 242	181.7 30.6 15.1	1949	Beverley	Cost £115,591 to build. Sold 13.7.1962 to Henriksen & Co. Ltd., Hull for £157,000 renamed *Miletus*. Scrapped in 1969 at Blyth.
Swanella (1)	H42	684 246	181.7 30.6 15.1	1949	Beverley	Cost £102,794 to build. Sold 3.3.1952 to the Firth Steam Fishing Co. a subsidiary of Thomas Hamling & Co. Hull for £145,000, renamed *St. Amant*. Scrapped in 1973 A. Draper & Son Ltd. Hull.
Bulby	FD147	360 139	136.1 25.2 13.2	1946	Beverley	Bought 27.7.1949 from the Seddon Fishing Co. London, for £40,280. Sold 27.12.1953 to the National Trawling & Fishing Co. Cape Town for £46,750. Scuttled in 1968 at False Bay Cape Town, one of several ships used to form an artificial reef.
Andradite	H26	312 139	131.0 24.6 13.0	1934	Beverley	Bought 23.2.1949 from Kingston Steam Trawling Co. Hull for £30,250. Wrecked 7.3.1957 in Castlebay, Barra, Outer Hebrides. All crew saved.
Alexandrite	H7	312 139	131.0 24.6 13.0	1934	Beverley	Bought 23.2.1949 from Kingston Steam Trawling Co. Hull for £30,250. Sold 4.12.1951 to the North Star Fishing Co. Aberdeen for £29,000. Scrapped in 1963.

Achroite H81 1949-1959.

Northella (2) *H159 1950-1956.*

Farnella (2) ex *Junella (2)* H399 1951-1966.

Velia (3) H239 = FD116 1952-1964.

NAME	P.L.N.	GROSS NET TONS	LENGTH BREADTH DEPTH	YEAR BUILT	BUILDER PLACE	NOTES
Achroite	H81	313 137	133.2 24.5 12.9	1934	Beverley	Bought 11.8.1949 from Kingston Steam Trawling Co. Hull for £72,500. Sold 1959, to the Cevic Steam Fishing Co. Fleetwood. Wrecked 2.1963 in severe weather on way to shipbreakers.
mv. *Lammermuir*	H105	729 265	190.7 32.3	1950	Aberdeen	Built as a joint venture between Boston Deep Sea Fisheries and J. Marr and Son Ltd. Sold 1956 to Faroese owners renamed *Jegvan Elias Thomsen*. Scrapped in 1976.
Westhawk x *Dalmatia* x *Lady Rosemary*	H474	360 142	140.4 24.0 13.2	1928	Beverley	Bought 22.9.1950 from the British Mutual Bank for £21,155. For use under the lay up scheme and fishing quotas. Sold 27.11.1952 to the British Iron & Steel Corporation for scrapping.
Westhill x *Larch* x *St. Alexander*	H470	360 140	140.4 24.0 13.2	1928	Beverley	Bought 22.9.1950 from the British Mutual Bank for £18,714. For use under the lay up scheme and fishing quotas. Sold 6.10.1952 to the British Iron & Steel Corporation for scrapping.
Reptonian x *St. Arcadius* x *Istrid* x *Basque*	H363 FD171	409 174	154.6 25.6 13.9	1933	Beverley	Bought 26.10.1950 from the Eton Fishing Co. Hull for £30,000. Sold 24.5.1951 to the Dinas Steam Trawling Co. for £39,625. Scrapped in 1959.
Northella (2)	H159	786 284	188.5 32.1 15.5	1950	Beverley	Cost £135,922 to build. Sold 1956 to Faroese owners for £178,000 renamed *Gullberg*. Sold 1965 to Henriksen & Co. Hull renamed *Calydon*. Scrapped in 1973 by A. Draper & Son Ltd., Victoria Dock, Hull.
Farnella (2) *Junella (2)* x *St. Crispin*	H399	558 201	170.8 29.2 14.2	1947	Beverley	Sister ship to the *Lorella*. Bought 5.7.1951 from the West Hartlepool Steam Navigation Co. for £108,412, renamed *Junella (2)*, in 1961 renamed *Farnella (2)*. Scrapped in 1966.
Rossella x *Hugh Walpole*	H336	498 192	166.7 27.6 14.2	1937	Selby	Bought 27.1.1951 from Newington Steam Trawling Co. for £60,321, renamed *Rossella* Sold 2.6.1959 for scrapping at Ghent.

NAME	P.L.N.	GROSS NET TONS	LENGTH BREADTH DEPTH	YEAR BUILT	BUILDER PLACE	NOTES
Bayella x *Cayton Bay*	H72	580 209	171.5 29.2 14.4	1952	Beverley	Bought 12.1.1952 from St. Andrew's Steam Fishing Co. Hull for £119,886, renamed *Bayella*. Sold 26.9.1966 for scrapping at Ghent.
Arctic Trapper x *Forbes* x *Coral Island* x *Alexander Hills*	H567	324 149	138.5 23.7 12.8	1917	Selby	Bought 7.3.1952 from Boyd Line Ltd., Hull for £8,000. For use under the lay up scheme and fishing quotas. Sold 6.10.1952 to the British Iron & Steel Corporation for scrapping.
Kirkella (2)	H209	790 285	190.2 32.1 15.7	1952	Beverley	Cost £160,033 to build. Sold 31.3.1963 to Boyd Line Ltd. Hull for £108,000, renamed *Arctic Galliard*, renamed *Arctic Outlaw* in 1973. Scrapped in 1974 in Spain.
mv. *Hildina (2)*	H222	296 102	128.2 26.6 12.2	1952	Beverley	Lost 1.12.1953 capsized in rough seas north of Scotland after the trawl had caught fast on the seabed. She had just transferred to Fleetwood. Six crew were lost.
mv. *Velia (3)*	FD116 H239	296 102	128.2 26.6 12.2	1952	Beverley	Cost £82,438 to build. Sold 18.7.1964 to Giacalone ela Pasea Sicily for £51,000. Renamed *Salvatore Giacalone*. Still in service fishing out of Mazara del Valio, Italy.
mv. *Irvana (2)*	FD152	296 102	128.2 26.6 12.2	1953	Beverley	Cost £81,609 to build. Stranded 23.4.1964 in Cushenden Bay, Northern Ireland, the *Irvana* was subsequently refloated but declared a total loss and sold 5.6.1964 to Shipbreaking Industries Ltd. for scrap.
mv. *Idena (2)*	FD136	296 102	128.2 26.6 12.2	1953	Beverley	Cost £86,032 to build. Sold 20.7.1967 to P. & J. Johnstone Aberdeen for £42,000. Sold 1974 to Putford Enterprises Ltd., Lowestoft for use as a standby safety vessel renamed *Falkirk*. In 1979 renamed *Grampian Falcon*. In 1987 converted to an auxiliary sailing vessel named *Miami Clipper*. Still in service owned by Bon Voyage Enterprise Inc.

Brucella H291 1953-1977.

Marbella (1) H52 1955-1965.

Dorinda FD22 1955-1978.

Swanella (2) H141 1957-1962.

NAME	P.L.N.	GROSS NET TONS	LENGTH BREADTH DEPTH	YEAR BUILT	BUILDER PLACE	NOTES
mv. *Gavina (2)*	FD167 A871	315 109	127.7 26.6 12.3	1953	Selby	Cost £84,167 to build. Sold 1964 to the Dinas Steam Fishing Co. Sold 20.7.1967 to P. & J. Johnstone Aberdeen, for £40,000. Scrapped in 1971.
mv. *Luneda (2)*	FD175 A754	315 109	127.7 26.6 12.3	1953	Selby	Cost £84,275 to build. Sold 1964 to P. & J. Johnstone Aberdeen. Scrapped in 1971.
mv. *Brucella*	H291	677 248	175.1 31.6 14.2	1953	Beverley	Cost £185,375 to build. The Company's first deepwater motor trawler. This highly successful vessel was retained by the Company all its working life. Sold 21.2.1977 to Albert Draper & Sons Hull for scrapping at the Victoria Dock slipway.
Lancella	H290	790 285	190.2 32.1 15.7	1953	Beverley	Cost £170,067 to build. Won the 1956 Silver Cod Trophy, with skipper Bill Turner. Retained by the Company all her working life. Scrapped in 1974 at Blyth.
Curtana	GY369	354 149	140.2 24.6 13.3	1929	Beverley	Bought 21.8.1953 from the Loyal Steam Fishing Co. Grimsby for £9,000. For use under the lay up scheme and fishing quotas. Sold 1.4.1954 to J. W. Draper & Sons Ltd. Grimsby for scrapping.
Sicyon	GY376	344 154	140.2 24.6 13.2	1930	Beverley	Bought 21.8.1953 from the Standard Steam Fishing Co. Grimsby for £9,000. For use under the lay up scheme and fishing quotas. Sold 1.4.1954 to J. W. Draper & Sons Ltd. Grimsby for scrapping.
Glenella x *Etonian* x *Cape Barfleur*	H333	473 187	161.0 26.6 14.2	1934	Selby	Bought 2.3.1954 from Eton Steam Fishing Co. Hull for £27,250 renamed *Glenella*. Sold 13.5.1957 to the British Iron & Steel Corporation for scrapping.
George Hastings x *Loch Leven*	FD9	357 154	140.4 24.0 14.8	1928	Beverley	Bought 4.5.1954 from the Dinas Steam Trawling Co. Fleetwood for £7,700. Sold 1.6.1954 to the British Iron & Steel Corporation for scrapping at Llanelly.

NAME	P.L.N.	GROSS NET TONS	LENGTH BREADTH DEPTH	YEAR BUILT	BUILDER PLACE	NOTES
Lady Enid x *Lyness* x *St. Amant* x *John Jefferson*	FD4	324 131	138.5 23.7 12.8	1918	Selby	Bought 4.5.1954 from the Dinas Steam Trawling Co. Fleetwood for £7,000. Sold 1.6.1954 to the British Iron & Steel Corporation for scrapping.
Red Charger x *Arkwright*	LO460	369 149	243.6 24.5 13.2	1930	Beverley	Bought 28.3.1955 from the Iago Steam Trawling Co. Fleetwood. Sold 4.1955 for scrapping.
Marbella (1)	H52	792 278	190.2 32.10 15.7	1955	Beverley	Sold 1.12.1965 to Boyd Line Ltd. Hull for £124,000. Renamed *Arctic Brigand*. Sailed from Hull 4.7.1975 for scrapping at Zeebrugge.
Thornella (2)	H84	792 278	190.2 32.10 15.7	1955	Beverley	Top earning British trawler in 1956 landed fish valued at £129,563. Retained by Company all her working life. Scrapped in 1973 on the Tyne.
Spurnella x *Stella Pegasi* x *Marath* x *Lord Ancaster* x *Wolborough*	H414	458 173	175.5 27.1 15.8	1937	Middlesbro'	Bought 24.9.1955 from Charleson Smith Ltd., renamed *Spurnella*. Sold 14.8.1958 to the Dinas Steam Trawling Co. Sold 16.6.1959 to Heward Trawlers Ltd., Fleetwood. Sailed 20.12.1962 for scrapping at Barrow.
mv. *Collena (2)*	FD20	334 113	132.5 26.7 11.7	1955	Selby	This class of trawler cost around £125,000 to build. Renamed *Velia* in 1963. Scrapped in 1972.
mv. *Jacinta (2)*	FD21	334 113	132.5 26.7 11.7	1955	Selby	Built for the City Fishing Co. Transferred 1969 to the Bon Accord Steam Fishing Co. Aberdeen. Scrapped in 1971.
mv. *Dorinda (2)*	FD22	334 113	132.5 26.7 11.7	1955	Selby	Converted in 1975 to a standby safety vessel. Sold 1978 to World Wide Surveys, Panama. Still in service.
Swanella (2)	H141	823 288	190.7 32.10 16.6	1957	Beverley	Last steamer built for the Company's fleet. Sold 13.7.1962 to Henriksen & Co. Ltd., Hull for £157,000 renamed *Tarchon*. Sold 1973 to Newington Trawlers Hull renamed *Rudyard Kipling*. Sold 11.1974 for scrapping in Spain.

Josena FD150 1957-1984.

Northella (3) H98 1958-1978.

Corena (2) FD173 1959-1970.

NAME	P.L.N.	GROSS NET TONS	LENGTH BREADTH DEPTH	YEAR BUILT	BUILDER PLACE	NOTES
mv. *Lucida (3)*	H403 FD437	392 141	138.2 27.6 11.6	1957	Beverley	Transferred to Hull. Sold 11.1.1980 to Albert Draper & Sons Hull for scrapping.
mv. *Josena (2)*	FD150	392 141	138.2 27.6 11.6	1957	Beverley	Converted in 1975 for standby safety work. Sold 1984 to Christ Compania Nav. SA. Panama renamed *Cormoran*. Still in service.
mv. *Edwina (2)*	FD162	392 141	138.2 27.6 11.6	1958	Beverley	Converted in 1975 to a standby safety vessel. Sold 1984 to G.L.A.D. Lines, Panama. Still in service.
mv. *Northella (3)*	H98	789 288	189.9 33.6 14.7	1958	Beverley	Won the 1961 Silver Cod Trophy with skipper Charles Drever. Renamed *Primella* in 1963. Won the 1968 Silver Cod trophy and the Distant Water Challenge Shield with skipper Bill Wilson. Sold 5.4.1978 to Albert Draper & Sons Hull for scrapping.
mv. *Benella (2)*	H132	789 289	189.9 33.6 14.7	1959	Beverley	Cost £267,000 to build. Last of the Company's side fishing trawlers to remain in service. Converted to a standby safety vessel in 1977. Sold 1991 to Cam Shipping Grimsby. Sailed 15.11.1993 from Grimsby for scrapping on the Thames.
mv. *Corena (2)*	FD173	352 124	132.9 27.1 12.2	1959	Selby	First trawler to have a variable pitch propeller. Sold 1970 to Ranger Fishing Co. Aberdeen. Sold 1976 to Colne Shipping Lowestoft for use as a standby safety vessel renamed *Trinidad*. Sold 31.1.1987 to Liguria Maritime Ltd., for scrapping at Sittingbourne.
mv. *Navena (2)*	FD172	352 124	132.9 27.1 12.2	1959	Selby	Sold 28.1.1969 to P. & J. Johnstone, Aberdeen. Wrecked 6.12.1973 on Copinsay, Orkney.
mv *Dinas (3)*	FD55	439 155	139.8 28.2 13.1	1956	Selby	Bought 1959, from the Dinas Steam Fishing Co. Transferred to Aberdeen in 1969. Sold 4.1976 to Albert Draper & Sons Ltd., Hull for scrapping.

NAME	P.L.N.	GROSS NET TONS	LENGTH BREADTH DEPTH	YEAR BUILT	BUILDER PLACE	NOTES
mv. *Westella (3)*	H194	778 275	189.7 33.6 14.3	1960	Beverley	Sold 22.11.1978 to Paul Franklin Watson, Vancouver renamed *Sea Shepherd* for use in the study and protection of marine creatures. Scuttled 3.1.1979 off Spain after an incident involving a collision with the pirate whaler *Sierra*, which was later sunk by a limpet mine whilst in harbour.
mv. *Starella (2)*	H219	606 207	165.0 30.10 16.3	1960	Beverley	Last side fishing trawler built for the Company's Hull fleet cost £209,000 to build. Sold 1975 to Boyd Line Ltd., Hull renamed *Arctic Rebel*. The last Hull trawler to fish at Iceland before the exclusion came into force. Sold 1.5.1979 to Colne Shipping Lowestoft for conversion to standby safety vessel renamed *St. Matthew*. Sold 16.12.1986, to K. & M. Davies for scrapping at Milford Haven.
mv. *Lavinda*	FD159 A742	262 97	118.2 25.1 11.1	1960	Selby	Sold 14.4.1964 to Richard Irvin, North Shields for £24,000 renamed *Ben Arthur*. Sold 1971 to Icelandic owners renamed *Freyja*. Sold 1975 renamed *Arsaell Sigurdsson*. Scrapped in 1983.
mv. *Arlanda*	FD206	431 153	139.8 28.0 12.10	1961	Selby	Built for the City Steam Fishing Co. Sold 1974 to the Cevic Steam Fishing Co. Converted 1975 to a standby safety vessel. Sold 1978 to Kaleawo Enterprises, Tema, Ghana renamed *Tohale*. Scrapped in 1992.
mv. *Armana (2)*	FD207	437 151	139.6 28.0 14.3	1962	Goole	Sold 1969 to Irvin & Johnson, Cape Town Still fishing owned by Viking Fishing Co. Pty Cape Town, South Africa.
mv. *Junella (3)* Freezer	H347	1435 588	240.7 38.7 26.3	1962	Aberdeen	The first British wholefish freezer trawler Sold 1973 to the Atlantic Trawling Pty, Cape Town, South Africa renamed *Bluefin*. Sold 1977 renamed *Southern Ranger*. Still fishing owned by Atlantic Fishing Enterprises, Cape Town, South Africa.

Lavinda FD159 1960-1964.

Arlanda FD206 1961-1978.

Kirkella (3) H367 1965-1984.

Criscilla (2) FD261 1966-1979.

NAME	P.L.N.	GROSS NET TONS	LENGTH BREADTH DEPTH	YEAR BUILT	BUILDER PLACE	NOTES
mv. *Northella (4)* Freezer	H301	1718 696	245.6 40.6 26.6	1964	Aberdeen	Sold 1973 to the Atlantic Trawling Pty, Cape Town, South Africa renamed *Yellowfin*. Sold 1977 renamed *Southern Fighter*. Sold for scrapping in 1992.
mv. *Kirkella (3)* Freezer	H367	1714 694	245.6 40.6 26.6	1965	Aberdeen	Last of the Company's first generation of freezers to remain in the fishing role. Sold 1984 to Seaboard Offshore Ltd., Inverness converted to a standby safety and fire-fighting vessel. Renamed *Seaboard Implacable*. Still in service.
mv. *Maretta (2)*	FD245	439 149	135.2 28.4 14.6	1965	Beverley	A top Fleetwood trawler in her class with skipper Sid Christy. Sold 7.6.1977 to Kale-alo Enterprises, Tema, Ghana. Renamed *Madden Marr*. Wrecked in 1979 off Ghana.
mv. *Zonia*	FD236	440 149	135.2 28.4 14.6	1965	Beverley	This class of trawler cost £169,000 to build. A top Fleetwood trawler in her class with skipper Victor Buschini. Sold 1977 to Boyd Line Ltd., Hull renamed *Arctic Brigand*. Sold 1979 renamed *Grampian Hunter*. Sold 1987 renamed *Stella Orion*. Still in service as a standby safety vessel.
mv. *Criscilla (2)* Freezer	FD261	952 411	185.6 36.1 23.0	1966	Aberdeen	The only freezer stern trawler built to operate out of the port of Fleetwood. Later transferred to Hull. Sold 27.7.1979 to the Royal Aircraft Establishment, Farnboro' for use as a research survey vessel. Renamed *Colonal Templer*. Still in service.
mv. *Marbella (2)* Freezer	H384	1786 718	245.6 40.7 26.6	1966	Goole	The *Marbella* was the top British freezer in 1967, landing 3,784 tonnes of fish, equal to 60,544 kits. On 22.11.1979 *Marbella* sailed to Middlesbrough to be converted for seismographic survey work and was renamed *Northern Horizon*. Still in service.

NAME	P.L.N.	GROSS NET TONS	LENGTH BREADTH DEPTH	YEAR BUILT	BUILDER PLACE	NOTES
mv. *Swanella (3)* Freezer	H421	1779 714	247.9 40.8 26.6	1967	Goole	In 1969 *Swanella* was the Company's top trawler landing an impressive 4,102 tonnes of fish. Sold 12.6.1981 to Kaare Misje & Co. Bergen for use as a diving support ship. Renamed *Archimedes*. In 1985 renamed *Drive Performer*. Still in service named *Seaway Commander*, Bergen Norway.
mv. *Glenstruan*	A200	183 62	106.2 23.4 11.8	1958	Peterhead	Bought 1968 from P. & J. Johnstone Aberdeen. Sold 1976 to Warbler Fishing Co. Aberdeen converted to a standby safety vessel. In 1981 renamed *Dawn Gem*. Present owners Cromwell Trust, Aberdeen. Still in service.
Loch Kildonan	A84	149 50	92.2 22.6	1956	Buckie	Bought 1968 from P. & J. Johnstone Aberdeen. Sold 1975 to M. P. Buchan & others, Peterhead. Sank 17.1.1987 in position 58.55 N x 00.28 E whilst in tow, crew abandoned vessel after she started taking in water.
Radiation (Wood)	A115	139 59	93.9 22.11 11.4	1957	Anstr.	Bought 1968 from P. & J. Johnstone, Aberdeen. Sold to R. M. Patrick & others. Still in service until 1992-93. Now delisted.
Paramount	A309	250 80	115.4 25.4 8.0	1959	Gateshead	Bought 1968 from P. & J. Johnstone, Aberdeen. Sold 1984 to Putford Enterprises Ltd. Aberdeen. Converted to a standby safety vessel and renamed *Putford Eagle*. In 1986 converted back to fishing and renamed *Pitufo* owned by Interpesco U.K. Ltd. Still in service.
Partisan	A310	250 80	115.4 25.4 8.0	1959	Gateshead	Bought 1968 from P. & J. Johnstone, Aberdeen. Converted in 1975 to a standby safety vessel. Sold 1983 to Albert Draper & Sons, arrived at Victoria Dock slipway for scrapping on 15.4.1983.
Forward Pride	A367	215 71	106.1 24.4 11.9	1960	Peterhead	Bought 1968 from P. & J. Johnstone, Aberdeen. Sold 1973 to Argentinian owners renamed *Antonio Manuel*. Present owners Filemar S.R.L. Still fishing from Mar Del Plata, Argentina.

Marbella (2) H384 1966-.

Partisan A310 1968-1983.

Southella (2) H40 1969-.

Gavina (3) FD126 1971-1985.

NAME	P.L.N.	GROSS NET TONS	LENGTH BREADTH DEPTH	YEAR BUILT	BUILDER PLACE	NOTES
Forward Grace	A531	212 68	106.1 24.4 11.9	1961	Peterhead	Bought 1968 from P. & J. Johnstone, Aberdeen. Sold 1973 to Argentinian owners renamed *Alberto R.* Present owners Filemar S.R.L. Still fishing from Mar Del Plata, Argentina.
Coastal Emperor	A456	250 81	115.4 25.3 8.0	1960	Gateshead	Bought 1968 from P. & J. Johnstone, Aberdeen. Converted in 1978 to a standby safety vessel. Driven ashore 6.12.1978 4 miles north of Aberdeen. Scrapping began in 1980 where she went aground.
Coastal Empress	A455	250 81	115.4 25.3 8.0	1960	Gateshead	Bought 1968 from P. & J. Johnstone, Aberdeen. Sank 12.5.1977 off Muckle Flugga following a collision with the 276 ton Faroese trawler *Nordingur*.
Jacamar	A525	237 67	115.4 25.4 11.0	1961	Appledore	Bought 1968 from P. & J. Johnstone, Aberdeen. Converted to a standby safety vessel in 1975. Sold 1981 to Warbler Fishing Co. for use as a standby safety vessel. Renamed *Dawn Monarch.* Still in service 1992. Out of class 1994.
mv. *Southella (2)* Freezer	H40	1144 382	246.0 41.8 26.6	1969	Aberdeen	The *Southella* was the top British freezer in 1971, landing 2,574 tonnes of fish. *Southella*'s fine hull design was used by the Royal Navy for their Castle Class Fishery Patrol vessels. In 1981 *Southella* sailed to Immingham to be converted to a seismographic survey vessel renamed *Seismella.* In 1986 whilst on charter to the Falkland Islands renamed *Falklands Desire.* Still in service.
mv. *Rosa Maris (2)*	FD284	109 39	76.4 21.0 9.5	1970	Thorne	An inshore trawler. Sold 1973 to J. N. Ward Fleetwood renamed *Rosamonda.* Still fishing owned by J. L. Banks, Fleetwood.
mv. *Merrydale (2)*	FD104	145 44	88.5 21.7 10.9	1970	Thorne	Inshore stern trawler. Sold 1973 to J. N. Ward, Fleetwood renamed *Resound.* Still fishing named *Arianna Premir* from Valetta, Malta.

NAME	P.L.N.	GROSS NET TONS	LENGTH BREADTH DEPTH	YEAR BUILT	BUILDER PLACE	NOTES
mv. *Cevic (3)*	FD241	249 81	116.3 25.4 11.3	1958	Lowestoft	Taken over 1970 when J. Marr acquired the Cevic Steam Fishing Co. Converted to a standby safety vessel in 1976. Sold 1978 to George Craig, Aberdeen renamed *Grampian Ranger*. Sold 7.1986 to D. Deck for scrapping at Plymouth.
mv. *Gavina (3)*	FD126	532 180	137.1 32.1 12.10	1971	Wallsend	First in a highly successful class of wetfish stern trawler. Transferred to Hull 1982. Sold 1985 to Cam Shipping Co. Converted to a standby safety vessel renamed *Cam Searcher* still in service.
mv. *Luneda (3)*	FD134	532 178	137.1 32.1 12.10	1971	Wallsend	Transferred to Hull in 1982. Sold 1985 to Cam Shipping Co. Converted to a standby Safety vessel renamed *Cam Guardian* still in service.
mv. *Irvana (3)*	FD141	533 178	137.1 32.1 12.10	1972	Grangemouth	Transferred to Hull in 1982. Sold 1985 to Cam Shipping Co. Converted to a standby safety vessel renamed *Cam Retriever* still in service.
mv. *Jacinta (3)*	FD159	599 178	142.8 32.1 12.10	1972	Wallsend	Transferred to Hull in 1982. In February 1990 the *Jacinta* with skipper Dennis Beaumont set up a British record catch of £270,516. Left Hull 9.2.1995 under tow for Fleetwood to become the focal point of a maritime museum.
mv. *Fyldea (2)*	FD182	582 218	142.8 32.1 12.10	1973	Wallsend	Sold 29.12.1978 to Bonasvista Coldstore Co. St. John's Newfoundland renamed *Fermeuse*. Still in service.
mv. *Glen Affric*	A175	114 40	79.8 21.7 10.9	1971	Aberdeen	Sold 1981 to M. R. Keillor, Hull renamed *Helen Keillor*. Sold 1983 to P. & J. Johnstone, renamed *Fairline*. Still in service.
mv. *Glen Esk*	A184	114 40	79.8 21.7 10.9	1971	Aberdeen	Sold 1981 to J. T. Abbey, Hull renamed *Alcarondas*. Sold 1984 to P. & J. Johnstone converted to a seiner renamed *Dykarlyn*. Still in service.

Northella (5) H206 1973-.

Glen Moriston A238 1975-1983.

NAME	P.L.N.	GROSS NET TONS	LENGTH BREADTH DEPTH	YEAR BUILT	BUILDER PLACE	NOTES
mv. *Farnella (3)* Freezer	H135	1469 518	230.3 41.8 26.7	1973	Wallsend	The first of three sister ships built by Clelands. Served as a minesweeper with the Royal Navy during the Falklands War in 1982. In 1984 converted to hydrographic geophysical survey vessel. Still in service named *Northern Prince* owned by J. Marr Shipping.
mv. *Cordella (2)* Freezer	H177	1450 427	230.3 41.7 26.7	1973	Wallsend	Served with the Royal Navy during the Falklands War in 1982. Flagship of the *Cordella* group. Sold 1985 to Skeggs Seafoods, Nelson, New Zealand. Bought back 16.10.1992 by J. Marr Shipping. Still in service.
mv. *Northella (5)* Freezer	H206	1238 441	230.4 41.8 26.7	1973	Wallsend	Served with the Royal Navy during the Falklands War in 1982. In 1983 chartered by the M.O.D. Navy for use as a training ship. Still in service. Owned by J. Marr Shipping.
mv. *Collena (3)*	FD221	309 113	101.0 27.0 15.9	1973	Hessle	Renamed *Glen Rushen* in 1979. Renamed *Omega B* in 1987. Jointly owned by Andrew Marr International and V. Buschini. Still in service.
mv. *Velia (5)*	FD220	309 113	101.0 27.0 15.9	1973	Hessle	Renamed *Glen Helen* in 1979. Sold in 1989 to Suid-Oranje Visserye, Cape Town renamed *Suiderkus*. Still in service.
mv. *Glen Coe*	A283	299 113	106.7 27.5 15.7	1973	Goole	Sold June 1992 to the Jade Fishing Co. Canada. Still fishing from New Westminster B.C. Canada.
mv. *Glen Moriston*	A238	299 113	106.4 27.5 15.7	1973	Wallsend	Sold 1982 to Utgardur H/F, Iceland renamed *Haforn*. Renamed *Krossnes* in 1987. Capsized and sank 23.2.1992 off the north west coast of Iceland. 3 crewmen were lost.
mv. *Glen Carron*	A427	235 150	106.4 27.5 15.7	1974	Wallsend	Sold 1982 to Heimaskagi H/F Iceland renamed *Skipaskagi*. Still fishing named *Thuridur Halldorsdottir* from Vogar, Iceland.

NAME	P.L.N.	GROSS NET TONS	LENGTH BREADTH DEPTH	YEAR BUILT	BUILDER PLACE	NOTES
mv. *Glen Urquhart*	A364	299 113	106.7 27.3 15.7	1974	Goole	Sold 1982 to Ufsastrand H/F Iceland renamed *Baldur*. Still fishing named *Thor* from Hafnarfjordur, Iceland.
mv *Junella (4)*	H294	1614 601	198.8 43.1	1975	Wallsend	The last freezer stern trawler built for the British fleet. Served with the Royal Navy as a minesweeper during the Falklands War in 1982. Sold 29.6.1983 to Qarsorsaq Fiskeriseisrab, Godthab, Greenland. Sold 1987 to Stan Marr, Falkland Islands renamed *Hill Cove*. 1992 name reverted to *Junella*, operated by Fripur, Montevideo, Uruguay. Still in service.
mv. *Norina (2)*	FD324	387 145	39.30m 9.68 3.78	1975	Goole	Transferred to Hull in 1982. Still part of the Company's present fishing fleet.
mv. *Idena (3)*	FD325	387 145	39.30m 9.68 3.80	1976	Goole	Transferred to Hull in 1982. Still part of the Company's present fishing fleet.
mv. *Armana (3)*	FD322	393 156	39.58m 8.51 3.50	1976	Hull	The *Armana* with skipper Malcolm Trott was the first trawler to gross over £1 million in a calendar year. Sold 1994 to Donegal Deep Sea Fishing Co. Ltd. Eire.
mv. *Navena (3)*	FD323	393 156	39.58m 8.51 3.50	1976	Beverley	Last of the Company's ships to be built at Beverley. Stranded 27.1.1984 after being abandoned following an ingress of seawater into the factory deck, beached at Scarborough where she capsized. Subsequently sold Reyner Shipping Co. Still registered as a fishing vessel owned by S. & S. Sunderland Marine Ltd.
mv. *Glen Cova*	A607	168 58	27.39m 7.27 3.58	1976	Woolwich	Converted to a long liner in 1978. Sold 1980. In 1986 renamed *Grand Banker*. Still fishing from St. John's Newfoundland owned by John Cabot Ltd.

NAME	P.L.N.	GROSS NET TONS	LENGTH BREADTH DEPTH	YEAR BUILT	BUILDER PLACE	NOTES
mv. *Glen Artney*	A715	115 40	26.09, 6.81 2.66	1977	Middlesbro'	Built for J. Marr Aberdeen. Sold 1982 renamed *Resilient*. Still in service fishing from Fraserburgh owned by I. W. Thomson.
mv. *Glen Farg*	A760	115 40	26.09m 6.81 2.66	1977	Middlesbro'	Built for J. Marr Aberdeen. Sold 1982 renamed *Vernal*. Still in service fishing from Peterhead. Owned by M. Forman & Partners.
mv *Gavina (4)* x *St. Patrick*	H24	475 142	39.71m 9.17 3.68	1975	Gt. Yarmouth	Bought 1986 from Colne Fishing Co. Lowestoft. Renamed *Gavina*. Sold 1989 back to Colne Shipping renamed *St. Patrick*. Converted to a standby safety vessel in 1990. Still in service owned by Karlsen Offshore (Caymen) Ltd.
mv. *Thornella (3)*	H96	555 166	38.64m 9.78 4.55	1988	Selby	First new trawler built for the Company's fleet for 12 years. Still fishing part of the Company's present fleet.
mv. *Lancella (2)*	H98	555 166	38.64m 9.78 4.55	1988	Seiby	On 26.1.1990 the *Lancella* with skipper Dave Wright achieved a British record grossing of £260,324 for a single trip. still fishing part of the Company's present fleet.
mv. *Swanella (4)* x *Voowaarts*	H142	788 304	59.59m 9.48 4.10	1975	Woubrugge	A pelagic freezer vessel. Bought 1988 from Voowaarts V.O.F. Holland. Owned by Swanella Ltd. This Company was sold to North Atlantic Fishing Co. in February 1993.
mv. *Marbella* x *King Jupiter* x *Wargram* x *Westella* x *Onderneming II*	H99	915 274	63.73m 10.14 4.95	1974	Leiden Holland	A pelagic freezer vessel. Bought 1989 from J. H. Fisheries Ltd., renamed *Marbella*. Still fishing part of the Company's present fleet.

NAME	P.L.N.	GROSS NET TONS	LENGTH BREADTH DEPTH	YEAR BUILT	BUILDER PLACE	NOTES
mv. *Petronella* x *My Joy* x *Petronella* x *Eben Haezer*	H171	224 117	36.10m 7.58 3.40	1980	Zaandam Holland	A beam trawler. Bought 1990 from F. W. S. Carter & Sons Ltd. Owned by the Hull Fishing Co. Ltd., a joint venture with the Marr Group main share holders. Sold 1992 to Carina Fishing Co. Ltd.
mv. *Southella* x *Myrefisk 1*	H240	1129 338	51.52m 11.51 5.70	1986	Fiekkefjord Norway	Bought 1990 from A/s Oksnesfisk, Norway. Renamed *Southella*. Still part of the Company's present fleet.
mv. *Swanella* x *Gudmunda Torfadottir* x *Olympe* x *Stamsund*	H1065	1195 358	53.10m 12.00 6.9	1989	Verksted Norway	Bought 1994 from Vinnslustodin H.F. Iceland. Renamed *Irvana* (temp.) Renamed *Swanella*. Part of the Company's present fleet.

Junella (4) H294 1975-1983.

NAME	P.L.N.	GROSS NET TONS	LENGTH BREADTH DEPTH	YEAR BUILT	BUILDER PLACE	NOTES
Starella x *Subsea 2* x *San Simone Secondo* x *Genepesca IXO-69*		1161 408	73.00m 11.03 4.62	1965	Venice	A submersible mother ship. Bought 17.4.1979 from Hill Samuel Leasing Co. Ltd. renamed *Starella*. Sold 10.2.1989 to New Holland Shipyard Ltd., for scrapping at New Holland.
Pacific Horizon x *Subsea 1* x *North Sea Hunter* x *Erich Ollenhaver*		1598 551	70.60 12.65 4.8	1964	Bremerhaven	A seismographic survey vessel. Leased 16.1.1981 from Ship Mortgage Finance Co. Ltd. renamed *Pacific Horizon*. Still in service Marr Vessel Management.
Swanella x *British Viking* x *Vickers Vicking* x *Dortmund* x *Danasbank* x *Hamburg*		1898 732	83.60m 13.64 5.48	1965	Bremerhaven	A submersible mother ship. Bought 30.6.1982 from Fairfield Industries Ltd. renamed *Swanella*. Sold 2.4.1984 to Scientific Exploration Society renamed *Sir Walter Raleigh*. Still in service named *Marine Explorer*, London.
Eastella x *G. A. Reay* x *Arctic Privateer*		999 315	69.30m 12.10 4.99	1968	Gdynia	A Fishery Research Vessel. Bought 28.6.1984 from the Ministry of Agriculture Fisheries and Food. In 1987 renamed *Falklands Right*, then renamed *Eastella* in the same year. In 1991 renamed *Falklands Protector*. Sold 4.5.1993 to Aquanymph Navigation Co. South Africa. Still in service named *Aquanymph*.
Brucella *Lancella* x *Anton Dohrn* x *Walter Herwig*		1943 891	83.34m 12.58 4.80	1963	Bremerhaven	A Fishery Research Vessel. Bought 31.7.1987 from the West German Government renamed *Lancella*. 1987 renamed *Falklands Right*. In 1991 renamed *Brucella*. Sold 9.2.1993 to the New Holland Shipyard Ltd. for scrapping at New Holland.
Criscilla x *Jura*		892 515	59.52m 11.08 4.38	1973	Aberdeen	A Fishery Patrol Vessel. Bought 6.4.1988 from the Ministry of Defence renamed *Criscilla*. Sold 6.12.1990 to the Government of Mauritania renamed *N'Madi*. Still in service.
HV Fox x *Fox*		1056 594	57.77m 11.46 3.82	1968	Lowestoft	A Survey Research Vessel. Bought 29.3.1989 from the Ministry of Defence renamed *HV Fox*. Still in service owned by J. Marr Shipping Ltd.

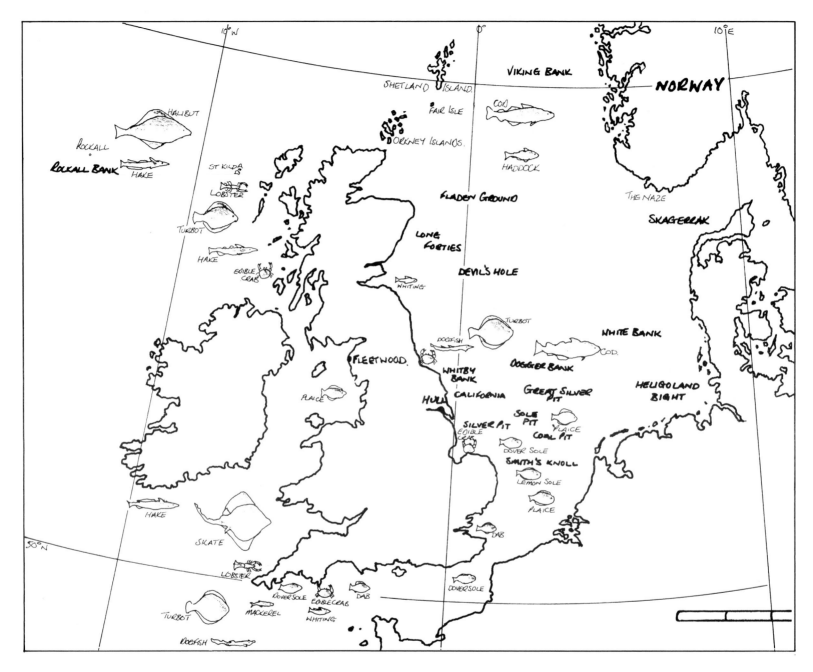

Map of Home Water Fishing Grounds.

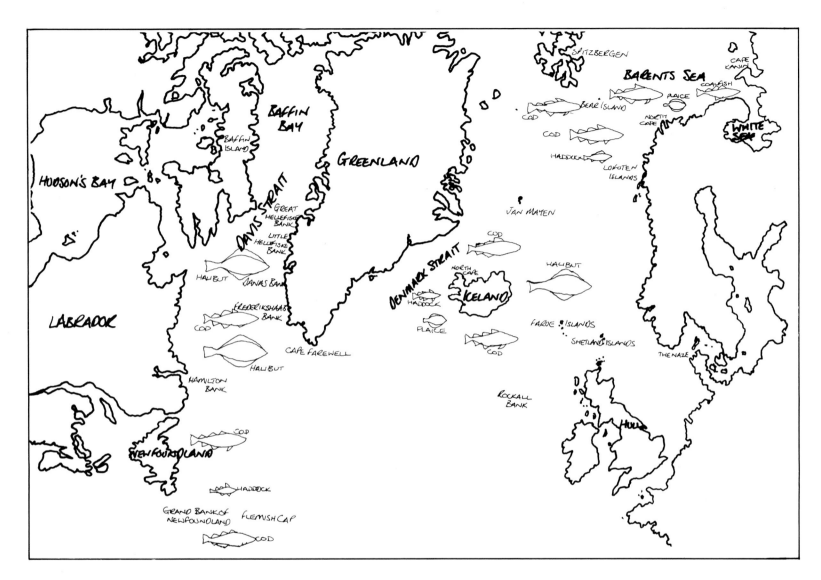

Map of Distant Water Fishing Grounds.

Who's Who

Ann Marr née Stephenson, wife of Joseph Marr.

Seven members of Joseph and Ann Marr's family circa 1900.
Back row left to right:
Edith Louise, Lillian Maud, Amy Isabel, James Herbert.
Front row left to right:
Joseph Arthur, Emily Florence, Rachel Anne.

The three sons of James Herbert Marr circa 1924, left to right:
Alan Marr, Geoffrey Edwards Marr and Leslie James Marr.

Marr's soccer team 1911-12 season. Taken on the North Eastern Football ground, Fleetwood, now the site of the Police Station and Magistrates Court.
Known members are: back row, 2nd left Sid Gardner (fish salesman), centre James Herbert Marr, in white Charlie Manning snr. 2nd right Alan Marr.
Front row, 2nd left Stan Quinn snr., with ball Fred Dollin (ship's husband), over his right shoulder Bill Tolner (stage foreman).

J. Marr & Son Ltd. staff outing to London May 10-12th 1929.

At a staff party in the 1930's, front row left to right: Mrs. Mackenzie, Mrs. Stella Marr, Leslie Marr, Mrs. Norah Marr, Geoffrey Marr and Mrs. Mary Ann Marr.

Mrs. Mackenzie (née E. M. Marr) being congratulated by her twin brothers, Mr. G. E. Marr (left) and Mr. Leslie J. Marr, after her wedding to Flight-Lieut. I. W. C. Mackenzie at Thornton Parish Church on 30th April 1935.

*Family group at the launch of **Northella** H159 at Beverley in 1949.*
Left to right: Geoffrey Edwards Marr, Caroline Marr, the nanny, Josephine Marr, a guest, G. Alan Marr, Mrs. Norah Marr,
(Mrs. G. E. Marr), Leslie James Marr.
Foreground, Andrew Marr, Georgina Marr.

Skippers and mates 1960's.
Left to right: William Drever,
G. Alan Marr, Charles Drever.
Two in the background unknown,
then Leslie Marr, Sid Morell,
Charles O'Neil and Bill Turner.

Mrs. G. Alan Marr the wife of the Company director launching the
*freezer stern trawler **Northella** H301 at Aberdeen on the 8th July 1964.*

149

At the launch of the M.T. **Gavina** *on 14th January 1971 are left to right:*
Mr. Andrew Leslie Marr, Mrs. A. L. Marr, (Else Lica), Mrs. Leslie Marr, (Stella), Mrs. G. A. Marr, (Margaret Rose Elisabeth),
and Mr. Geoffrey Alan Marr.

The launch of the freezer trawler Southella on 27th September 1968 at Hall Russell & Co. Shipyard, Aberdeen, by Mrs. Evelyn M. Mackenzie. Left to right: Mrs. Mackenzie (known as Girlie), Elizabeth Mackenzie, Stella Marr, Andrew Marr, Susan Marr, Josie Marr, G. Alan Marr, wife of G. Alan Marr, Margaret Marr, Managing Director of the Shipyard of Hall Russell, John Wright and Mrs. Wright.

Senior staff circa 1974. Left to right back row: Jimmy Mews, Sid Christie, Jim Carhill, Harold Helm, Jim Cross, Ronnie Puke, Irvin Clegg, Ron Buckton, John Kay. In the front row, seated: G. Alan Marr, Billy Sharp, Matt Sumner and Andrew L. Marr.

151

Dock visit in 1978.
Left to right: Roy Mason MP Minister of Fisheries, a visitor, Jim Johnson MP for West Hull,
Frank Knight and Charles Marr.

*In July 1978 whilst visiting the Hull and Grimsby Fish Docks, Prince Charles expressed an interest in making a voyage on a trawler. On 21st-23rd April 1980 the **Junella** played host to the Prince whilst fishing off the Hebridean coast. To the left of Prince Charles is trawler manager Charles Drever, Andrew Marr, Charles Marr, to his right James Marr and G. Alan Marr.*

Jim Cross retirement presentation in 1988. Left to right: Geoffrey Alan Marr, Charles Marr, Jim Cross.

Left to right: Peter Rose of Glenrose and Ted Cook who is the cousin of Margaret Marr, Ray Brookes and Geoffrey Alan Marr on the occasion of handing over a charitable cheque during Geoffrey Alan Marr's year as High Sheriff of Humberside.

Current Directors of the Marr Group of Companies – 1995 Back row left to right: Joseph Watson, David Gallacher, Alan Wilkinson, Nigel Atkins, Colin Clayton. Front row seated left to right: Charles Roger Marr, Margaret Rose Elisabeth Marr, Geoffrey Alan Marr, C.B.E. Chairman, James Geoffrey Marr, James Hind (separate photo).

FISHING GALLERY

*The crew of a steam trawler pose with
a good haul of hake circa 1910.*

*The deckies on the **Criscilla** gutting fish in the
pounds under the watchful eye of the mate, circa 1930.*

*A deckhand joins the **Northella** circa 1950, complete with a new pair of thigh boots from "stores".*
He is dressed in the traditional wide bottom trousers.

156

The Silver Cod winning trawler **Kirkella** *outward bound from St. Andrew's Dock, Hull.*

This photograph illustrates the hard work involved in shooting and hauling the gear of a side fishing trawler.

157

The chief engineer and his fireman at the controls of the steam trawler **Northella** *H159 circa 1950.*

*Aboard the **Swanella** H141 in April 1960. The mate supervises the emptying of the cod end seen with its protective covering of hides.*

With the foredeck full of fish the deckies and fishroom men face hours of hard work gutting and storing the catch. They will be fortified by the thoughts of good markets when they arrive back home.

Down in the fishroom a deckhand is laying out cod on shelves. Once a layer has been laid, shelf boards will be placed over the cod to prevent it being crushed by the weight of fish above it.

On arrival back in Hull, bobbers unload the catch which will be placed on the fish market to be sold at the early morning fish auction.

Bobbers at work unloading the **Junella** *H399 circa 1959.*

Filleter on the quayside processing the catch.

*Skipper Charles Drever hands out glasses of champagne to members of his crew aboard the **Northella** having received the news that they have won the 1961 Silver Cod trophy.*

*Skipper Charlie Taylor (top left), with members of his crew
on the **Kirkella** arrive back at Hull as the winners of the
1955 Silver Cod Challenge Trophy.*

*The Fleetwood trawler **Navena** FD172 steaming to the fishing grounds in the 1960's.*

*Families of the crew of the **Dinas** greet the trawler on its arrival back at Fleetwood in the 1960's.*

164

THE POWER OF THE SEA

*A watch keepers view from the bridge of the **Swanella** H141 in April 1960,*
whilst the trawler was dodging in heavy weather.

*The stricken trawler **Shackleton** aground at Rathlin Island, Northern Ireland.*
The photograph illustrates the difficulties the rescuers faced
in getting the 14 crewmen to safety.

On 1st March 1930 the **Shackleton** stranded on the rocks at Greenan Point during dense fog. The 14 crewmen of the stricken trawler were rescued by a team of men from Rathlin Island. In appreciation the Company erected a plaque and awarded the men scrolls.

The freezer stern trawler **Southella** H40 ships a sea up the ramp flooding the after deck whilst hauling its trawl. The deckies carry on with their duties being used to such occurrences.

On 9th January 1953, whilst homeward bound from the Greenland fishing grounds two Hull trawlers encountered severe weather conditions that could have resulted in their loss. The **Loch Moidart** and **Thornella** ran into a full North Easterly gale, whilst heading through an ice-strewn sea that compelled the vessels to turn and dodge into the wind.

When making a turn the **Loch Moidart** broached and a heavy sea swamped her flooding the bridge and radio room sweeping away her port lifeboat, ventilator, galley funnel and twisting the lifeboat davits.

The **Thornella** had cleared the ice when a huge wave came down on her crushing the bridge and flooding the radio room. Left with the steering gear barely hanging together and with only half a ship's wheel, skipper Charlie O'Neill navigated the vessel home with the aid of one of the lifeboat compasses. The radio operator James Cunningham persevered in drying out the radio equipment in the stokehold and managed to advise the trawler's owner that the vessel was safe. Both trawlers arrived home at St. Andrew's Dock on 17th January 1953.